Withdrawn from
Queen Margaret University Library

Not About

Ni ghtingales

ALSO AVAILABLE FROM METHUEN
BY THE SAME AUTHOR

A Streetcar Named Desire
(Methuen Student Edition)

Something Cloudy, Something Clear

for the complete catalogue
of Methuen Drama titles write to:

Methuen Drama
Random House
20 Vauxhall Bridge Road
London SW1V 2SA

TENNESSEE WILLIAMS

Not About Nightingales

EDITED, WITH AN INTRODUCTION, BY
ALLEAN HALE

FOREWORD BY
VANESSA REDGRAVE

METHUEN DRAMA

METHUEN MODERN PLAYS

Published by Methuen

2 4 6 8 10 9 7 5 3

First published in 1998 in Canada and USA by New Directions.
First published in the United Kingdom in 1998 by Methuen Drama,
Random House, 20 Vauxhall Bridge Road, London SW1V 2SA
and Australia, New Zealand and South Africa.

Not About Nightingales published by arrangement with The University of the South,
Sewanee, Tennessee.

Thanks are due to the Harry Ransom Humanities Research Center, The University
of Texas at Austin, where the original typescript is housed.

Special thanks are due to Thomas Keith for his help in preparing the manuscript.

Tennessee Williams' essay "The Timeless World of a Play," quoted in the Foreword, appeared in
the *New York Times*, January 14, 1951, and was then used as an introduction to the first published version of *The Rose Tattoo*, New Directions, 1951; it is now included in both *The Theatre of Tennessee Williams, Volume II* and *Where I Live: Selected Essays* (Copyright © 1951,
1971, 1978 by Tennessee Williams); used by permission of New Directions Publishing Corp.

Random House UK Limited Reg. No. 954009

A CIP catalogue record for this book
is available from the British Library

ISBN 0 413 72280 5

Text prepared in USA by New Directions Publishing Corp., New York
Printed and bound in Great Britain by Cox & Wyman Ltd, Reading, Berkshire

TABLE OF CONTENTS

FOREWORD

Fear and evasion are the two little beasts that chase
each other's tails in the revolving cage of our nervous
world. They distract us from feeling too much about
things. . . . So successfully have we disguised from
ourselves the intensity of our own feelings, the sensi-
bility of our own hearts, that plays in the tragic tradi-
tion have begun to seem untrue.

Tennessee Williams, 1951
"The Timeless World of a Play"

I first got to know Tennessee in 1980/81 when he wanted me
to play in a new script of his, *Stopped Rocking,* about a woman
who is incarcerated by her husband in a terrible mental institution. It was to be a film, but we couldn't get anyone interested, however, we did get to know each other.

Then, in April, 1982, he joined me for tea in the Ritz-
Carlton Hotel, by the side of Boston Common, and he could-
n't stop laughing. He had decided to join me in a single performance I had devised at the Orpheum Theatre, Boston, for
which he had chosen to read his essay, "Misunderstandings of
the Artist in Revolt." Tennessee was in a hilarious mood; close
friends had told him not to perform with me, but he had come
just the same. Also, it was in Boston, in December, 1940, that

the first night of his *Battle of Angels* got booed; the Boston City Council had adopted an order for an investigation of his play by an official censor, and the producers had summoned him to the Ritz-Carlton Hotel for a major rewrite, and had then taken the play off at the end of the Boston run. His dearest friend, Maria St. Just, told me that Tennessee always laughed in the theatre during really tragic scenes, so I think he was laughing fit to burst in April, 1982, because things seemed at that time just about as bad as they could be for both of us. In the winter of 88/89 Maria joined the rehearsals of Peter Hall's production of *Orpheus Decending* for Thelma Holt and Duncan Wheldon at the Theatre Royal, Haymarket. I was playing Lady Torrance. Tennessee had died four years previously and in his will had named Maria St. Just as executrix of his estate during her lifetime. Peter asked Maria to bring *Battle of Angels* to rehearsal. We read this, and wondered why the play had been so badly received in Boston; so badly that it had never been performed until 1957, when Harold Clurman directed the play *Orpheus Decending,* which is a rewrite of *Battle of Angels.*

Many people have asked me how I came to find *Not About Nightingales.* The answer is the simplest possible. I read the foreword Tennessee wrote, "The Past, the Present and the Perhaps" which was published in 1957, when *Orpheus Descending* was the hit of the Broadway season.

And so I drifted back to St Louis, again, and wrote my fourth long play which was the best of the lot. It was called *Not About Nightingales* and it concerned prison life, and I have never written anything since then that could compete with it in violence and horror, for it was based on something that actually occurred along about that time, the literal roasting alive of a group of intransigent convicts sent for correction to a hot room called "the Klondike."

In 1993 Corin Redgrave, Kika Markham and I founded our theatre company, Moving Theatre. I asked Maria again about *Not About Nightingales* which she had never read, and she promised to find the manuscript for me.

"There you are Tall Girl!" Maria exclaimed triumphantly, throwing the longed-for script onto her kitchen table at Gerald Road with one hand, while the other stretched to stir some delicious black soup made from mushrooms picked in the woods of "Wilbury." I gobbled the soup and the play, and I knew this had to be performed. The question remained, where and how, for *Not About Nightingales* is an ensemble piece requiring a large cast and a lot of rehearsal.

In early 1996, Moving Theatre moved to Texas to join the Alley Theatre, Houston, in an exciting repertory season of *Julius Caesar* and *Antony and Cleopatra*. Our association was built on an agreement that we would reciprocate the invitation and perform a play in London. We agreed that it would be appropriate, having performed the great English poet-dramatist, Shakespeare, to choose the unperformed play by the great American poet-dramatist, Williams.

I spent many hours at the Harry Ransom Humanities Research Center, The University of Texas at Austin, where Tennessee's earliest archives are kept, including the script which Maria had brought me. I would like to thank Cathy Henderson, the Research Librarian, and Melissa Miller of the Theatre Collection for all the help they gave me. There are thirteen large folders containing drafts and re-drafts of scenes from Tennessee's "work-bench" on *Not About Nightingales*. I found the rather summary rejection of the play from the Group Theatre. I also found many newscuttings from 1938 about the "Klondike" atrocity.

> One day late in August, 650 inmates of the Philadelphia County prison in Holmesberg, PA., struck against

a monotonous diet of hamburger and spaghetti, re-
fused their supper. Three days later the naked, tortured
bodies of four prisoners were found in an airtight cell.
They had been scalded to death.

An investigation was launched. Prison guards and
officers were arrested. The American public was
shocked to learn that "hot steam treatment" had been
given 25 unruly prisoners. A cry for "justice" arose.
But there is scant justice in most American prisons, and
county jails are generally the worst of the lot. . . .

—*Look* Magazine, 11 October, 1938

Newsweek reported in the September 5 issue:

Inside the walls of Philadelphia County's model
prison at Holmesburg, Pa., sits a small building re-
sembling a cowshed. Fifty feet long, 12 feet wide, and
8 feet high, it is ventilated only by three windows. Yet
this dingy brick structure, containing twelve barren 9
by 4 cells, is equipped with a bank of steam radiators
nearly sufficient to heat a baby skyscraper—six huge
ones of 50 coils each, capable of producing heat of 200
degrees, only 12 below the boiling point.

Into this oven last week were crowed 25 rebellious
prisoners, alleged ringleaders of a hunger strike. . . .
Windows had been closed; water in the cell basins had
been cut off by removal of the keys from the faucets.
. . . By morning the shrieks of torture had been
stilled. When guards opened Cell 6 and 7, where three
men had been huddled in each, two were dead in each
cell. They were Henry Osborn, Frank Comodeca, John
Walters, and James McQuade—victims of Holmesburg's dread "Klondike." . . . The result was a major
scandal, entangled in politics. When the deaths became

known city police were the first to investigate. They attempted to whitewash the incident, saying the victims had killed each other. But coroner Charles H. Hersch was skeptical and jumped in. First off he arrested two guards, then he sought the "higher-ups" believed to be responsible for one of the worst prison horrors in American history. But by the week's end he was making little progress amid what he labeled "a conspiracy of silence."

Tennessee's first title for the play was *The Rest is Silence: This play is dedicated to the memory of four men who died by torture in an American prison, August, 1938*. The draft he sent to the Group Theatre bore the name *Not About Nightingales*, a reference to the poem by John Keats which the prisoner, Canary Jim, reads in the play. This text was dedicated by Tennessee *For Clarence Darrow, the Great Defender, whose mental frontiers were the four corners of the sky*. I found two pencilled notes on two of the newscuttings: "If you think my play is melodramatic-Read This!" "And they say my play is melodramatic!"

It is now sixty years since the prisoners were killed and Tennessee wrote *Not About Nightingales*. Now Trevor Nunn is directing the play for the Royal National Theatre's co-production with Moving Theatre, in association with the Alley Theatre of Houston, Texas. Punishment is much in vogue again in Europe and in the United States. In Alabama and Texas chain-gangs have been reinstituted; we even see photographs of young women prisoners in forced-labor gangs. My brother, Corin, who plays the role of "Boss" Whalen, the Warden of the prison in the play, cut out a report in the British newspaper *The Independent* last autumn. Prison guards from the Hays State Prison in Georgia gave evidence of a "frenzied" beating of prisoners. Some naked, some shackled, the prisoners were kicked,

punched and stomped on, covering a thirty foot-long concrete
wall with their blood. A lawsuit was brought for some of the
prison inmates by the Southern Center for Human Rights. The
director of the Center, Stephen Bright, said: "It's not unusual to
have inmates telling you these things happen, what's remarkable is the verification of the guards."

So Tennessee was right when he wrote about the timeless
world of the play . . .

> A play may be violent, full of motion: yet it has that
> special kind of response which allows contemplation
> and produces the climate in which tragic importance is
> a possible thing, provided that certain modern condi-
> tions are met.

Vanessa Redgrave
January, 1998

INTRODUCTION: A CALL FOR JUSTICE

Not About Nightingales is remarkable not only as the work of a twenty-seven-year-old student named Thomas Lanier Williams, but as the first full-length play he signed as "Tennessee." The script lay in the Williams archives in the Harry Ransom Humanties Research Center at the University of Texas at Austin for more than fifty years until rescued by two British women. As you've just read in Vanessa Redgrave's Foreword, the Lady Maria St. Just, trustee of the Rose Williams Trust under Williams' will, showed the script to Ms. Redgrave, who was enthusiastic and arranged for its 1998 world premiere at the Royal National Theatre in London.

Written in 1938, the play shows us young Williams as a political writer, passionate about social injustice, a Williams who would have been quite at home with Britian's "angry young men" of two decades later. Yet it is a very American play in its reflection of the Great Depression of the thirties, its references to President Franklin D. Roosevelt's New Deal, its apprehension about Hitler and Mussolini and the approaching threat of war. The Depression was a controlling factor in Tom Williams' life. It forced him to quit the University of Missouri, where he had already won notice in literary contests, to work in a St. Louis shoe factory. His job was stupefying, typing orders eight hours a day, relieved only by stolen breaks to the washroom to write poetry on the lids of shoe boxes. He was reading Shelly and Keats, but was finding that real life was "not about nightingales." The factory years taught him what it meant to be a small wage-earner trapped in a hopelessly routine job. Home was no less an entrapment, with a father who despised him, parents in open warfare, and a beloved sister deteriorating into madness. He dreamed constantly of escape; entrapment and escape would become the theme of his early plays.

At age twenty-four a nervous breakdown freed him to return to school, this time at Washington University in St. Louis. There his best friend was an editor of *The Anvil, the Magazine of Proletarian Fiction,* a pseudo-Marxist publication which introduced such revolutionary writers as Richard Wright and Nelson Algren. Tom met the young writers who clustered around this magazine, radical activists working on federal relief projects, whose influence would strongly affect his writing. But his future as a playwright was determined when he encountered a dynamic theatre group called "The Mummers."

The credo of this committed band of actors was to deliver social plays with an emotional "punch," and when their director, Willard Holland, met Tom Williams, two like souls found each other. Tom's one previous full-length production was a comedy, *Cairo! Shanghai! Bombay!* performed by a neighborhood group. For the Mummers he wrote an antiwar piece, *Headlines,* as curtain-raiser for Irwin Shaw's powerful drama, *Bury the Dead.* By March of 1937, the Mummers produced his first long serious play, *Candles to the Sun,* about a miners' strike. A smashing success, it ended with the singing of "Solidarity Forever." Proletarian drama was the order of the day, and Odets' *Waiting for Lefty* was the seminal play. By December, the Mummers produced Williams' second long proletarian play, *Fugitive Kind.* Set in a flophouse on the St. Louis waterfront, it dealt with the big city's indifference to its outcasts. His third proletarian play would be conceived as a class assignment at the University of Iowa.

Iowa in 1937 was a mecca for would-be-playwrights. Its new theatre building was one of the best equipped in the United States, surpassing anything in New York; its curriculum emphasized playwriting based on performance. Iowa was strongly influenced by the Federal Theatre Project, since the head of playwriting, Edward C. Mabie, was one of the designers of that program. The Theatre Project was one of many Depression era plans under the Works Progress Administration (WPA), to provide jobs for the unemployed. It developed the "living newspaper" genre, a documentary style of drama in which scenes were tied together by projected headlines or an announcer. Since the headlines of the thirties concerned protest, poverty, and war, most of the "living newspaper" plays dealt with social issues.

The requirement in Tom's playwriting course, Experimental Dramatic Production, was to turn in a short play every two weeks based on a newspaper story; of these the three best would be given a workshop production. By October Tom wrote Holland: "I am having a play presented in the 'laboratory theater' next Thursday . . . a dramatization of the Hunger Strike among convicts at the Stateville Illinois prison—in protest against new parole policies which have reduced the number of paroles from over 1300 last year to about 240. . . ." Tom's very specific details are a puzzle: there seems to have been no hunger strike at Stateville since the riot of 1930 in which the prison was nearly destroyed. However, its parole system was the subject of a year-long investigation brought on by the murder of its most famous prisoner, Richard Loeb. This front-page story of January 29, 1936, was one Tom could not have missed. Loeb and Leopold, brilliant young men from wealthy Chicago families had, in 1924, executed "the crime of the century," a brutal child murder with no motive except the thrill of carrying out the perfect crime. They were saved from the death sentence by Clarence Darrow, the most famous criminal lawyer in America.

Tom called his Stateville sketch "Quit Eating" and filed it away as he pursued that year's other assignments, four more short plays, two full-length dramas and a group documentary on "Socialized Medicine." Recalling all the doctors who had expermented on his sister Rose, he wrote such a searing indictment that Professor Mabie tore up his paper. He had no better luck with the assignment to write a long autobiographical play. His offering, *Spring Storm*, a tragedy of young love, ended with the heroine stripping to the buff. The play was read in class to shocked silence. Mabie did not further Tom's application to pursue a graduate degree at Iowa. Tom Williams received his bachelor's degree in August, none of his family coming for the event. After two weeks in Chicago, trying to get on the WPA theatre project with no success, he returned home, jobless, penniless, feeling a loser. In St. Louis the Mummers had temporarily disbanded; his old friends were leaving for graduate school; his sister was in an asylum. His father made it clear that Tom was a parasite whose best hope was to be drafted. Deeply depressed, he thought increasingly of escape. Then on September 1, 1938, he read the news-story that would give him the way out.

In a high security prison in Holmesburg, Pennsylvania, twenty-five convicts who staged a hunger strike were locked into a steam-heated cell called "the Klondike." As the heat was turned up, four were literally roasted alive. America was horrified. Tom as usual expressed his feelings by writing. Enlarging his Iowa sketch of a hunger strike, "Quit Eating," he dramatized the Klondike massacre. As he wrote, he injected into the script some of America's shock and rage.

He first called his new version "Hell; An expressionistic drama based on the prison atrocity in Philadelphia County." By the end of September he was writing day and night on the script now called *Not About Nightingales*. It was his fourth long play and, he felt, the best of the lot. A routine of black coffee and sleeping pills kept him feeling like a volcano about to erupt, an explosiveness mirrored in the play. In mid-October a hope that the Mummers might produce it fell through, and he wrote in his journal that the script seems "pretty cheap stuff. . . ." A month later it seemed incredibly bad, and he felt quite desperate. By December he had finished the third draft, and put it away, unsure whether it was very good or very bad.

His description "expressionistic" is an important indication of William's intent. Although he would for years be branded as a realist, he was never truly that. He would always mix fantasy, even surrealism, with realism, as in the scene where Butch has a dream. His expressionistic techniques in this play—the psychological use of lighting, the contrast of dark and light suggesting prison bars, the groups marching or chanting in unison—are innovative examples. He did away with curtains, used lighting to mark scene changes and spots to enable simultaneous action on various parts of the stage. He introduced theme music, from jazz to Tchaikowsky, to express the characters' moods or comment satirically on the action. This is the most "living newspaper" of all Williams plays, using throughout the technique of an Announcer and caption titles for each scene. Announcements are extended to offstage reporting: shouted newspaper headlines, voices of broadcasters, sirens. Script directions of "theme up" and "fade-in," "fade-out" suggest that Tom may even have thought of projecting these titles on a scrim—as he would later suggest for *The Glass Menagerie*. While this Brechtian device implies techniques learned at Iowa, Tom had used captions in his two other proletarian plays before he heard of Brecht.

Not About Nightingales is notably the most cinematic of Williams' plays. It is written in twenty-two fluid, fast moving scenes called "Episodes," rather than the conventional three acts, although later he specified these as a concession to the commercial stage. At times the play seems better suited to the screen than to the stage in its quick dissolves, its opening flash forward and such effects as the pleasure boat passing by. It disregards logic, as convicts—supposedly in locked cells—are brought stage front and spotlighted for key speeches. The ending especially—Jim jumping out a prison window into the bay—can be realized visually in a film but is challenging to perform on stage. Perhaps Tom's innovative stage techniques were inspired by nothing more esoteric than the movies. "Going to the movies" had been his adolescent escape from home.

1937 was an especially big year for prison films and Tom had obviously been seeing them. At times his manuscript reads like a *film noir.* While most prison pictures had standard components—the tough convict, the cruel warden, conspiracy, riot, breakout, and gunfire—aspects of *Nightingales* point to a specific prize-winning film of 1935, *The Big House,* as inspiration. Is it significant that in it and *Nightingales* the "heavy" characters are both named "Butch"? Wallace Beery's prop in the film is a hidden knife; Tom's Butch has a concealed razor. Both film and play contain hunger strikes, though obviously Tom could not reproduce the film's dramatic climax where several hundred men seated at long tables start throwing food. Both have church scenes, but in Tom's they throw hymnbooks. The film's Butch invents a letter from a non-existent "Myrtle." Tom's Butch is given a romantic dream scene with "Goldie." The film's brief glimpse of bringing a man out of the Hole becomes the powerful and exciting Klondike scene of Williams' play as the men fight for life in the hissing steam. But it is the differences, not the likenesses, between *Nightingales* and the standard prison play or film that show Williams' originality. If this specific film was indeed a model for the apprentice playwright, he was already surpassing that model in dialogue and characterization. In the film, one is struck by the proper speech of the supposedly tough characters, who carefully pronounce their word endings, whereas the literate Tom writes street talk that is grittily real.

Most amazing is Tom's ability to imagine himself inside the skin of persons so unlike himself, a seemingly ordinary, shy, polite, middle-class young man. Although Tom's convicts have stock names—"Swifty," "the Canary," "The Queen,"—their speech and attitudes define them as more complex. He paints them with empathy, giving even his villain, the sadistic warden, two tender moments that make him human. Jim has aspirations but knuckles under when faced with consequences. Eva has some of the flirtatious quality of Blanche du Bois—she loves Jim, but is not totally unresponsive to the warden. Black Ollie is an unusual portrait for the time, more than a bit character or the comic Negro.

If Tom himself is in the play, it is in the character of Jim. In *Nightingales* Jim is described as smoking *à la Jules Garfield*. From his earliest one-acts to his final plays, Williams wrote with a specific actor in mind, whom he frequently mentioned by name. Apparently this helped him visualize the character. The fact that he calls Garfield "Jules," his real name, indicates an acquaintance with this actor's stage roles in the Group Theatre, the leftist avant-garde theatre in New York to which every young playwright aspired. Jules Garfield played in two of Odets' agitprop plays of the period, *Waiting for Lefty* and *Awake and Sing*, before going to Hollywood to become John Garfield. There he starred in a series of Warner Brothers films, including several prison movies. Tom evidently saw Garfield's 1938 film, *Four Daughters*, where, one review said, Garfield "outshone, outquipped and outsmoked every one in the cast." Perhaps Garfield was the ideal of what Tom would like to have been. Small like Tom, but exceedingly handsome, he had a brash, cocky style—the opposite of Tom's diffidence—and a masterful way with women. Garfield's film roles fit Tom's subject matter as well: the perpetual outsider, the tough guy who longs for the stars. Apparently Williams followed Garfield through the years, as Garfield was his first choice to play Stanley in *A Streetcar Named Desire*. (A role made famous by newcomer Marlon Brando.)

In Jim's lyrical passages, which stand out from the sardonic diction of his working class speech, it is Tom speaking: the deeply felt monologues, with references to being caged, to feeling the locked-up power that can cause revolutions. When Jim tears up Keats' "Ode to a Nightingale," Tom is saying the poet must turn activist. Jim's key monologue on guilt in the last episode of Act Two voices a theme Williams would repeat throughout his work: the conviction that man has no free will, therefore no guilt. Interestingly, this was the argument Clarence Darrow used in the Loeb-Leopold case, claiming that man is a product of three factors over which he has no control—heredity, environment, and chance. Tom dedicated his play to the champion of lost causes, Clarence Darrow, who died in 1938.

Of all Tom's characters, Eva is the least realized, the standard ingenue except for her lyrical outburst near the end. Williams had not yet learned to create his famous women and the rather awkward love story marks this as a youthful work. Although at Iowa he had had a tempestuous sexual affair with a woman, (described in his *Memoirs*) that fact is not reflected in this play. After this affair, and several failures to attract girls, he had given up on heterosexual love, feeling himself a loser with women as well. This play depicts his first homosexual—a minor character, but daring in the 1930s. Although in no sense a homosexual play, *Not About Nightingales* portrays the transvestite queen with accuracy and compassion. Tom would not find his own sexual identity until several years later.

One final element of this play is uniquely Williams: the tragicomic mix. Whereas *The Big House* is grim throughout,

Nightingales introduces two comic scenes that are gratuitous and personal. In "Sunday Morning in Hall C," Tom takes revenge on the St. Louis he hated, satirizing its society as dominated by a German brewer of ridiculous lineage. Augustus Busch Jr., of the Anheuser-Busch brewing family (makers of Budweiser beer), had founded the Bridlespur Hunt Club, whose wealthy members included a socialite "horsey set." Tom's own lineage was rather distinguished, as his mother never let him forget: descent from one Colonial governor of America, from the illustrious Coffin family, first settlers of New England, and from the founders of the State of Tennessee (with Civil War poet Sidney Lanier as a side branch on the family tree). Perhaps he is also poking fun at his mother, to whom social position and background were so important.

The scene of the two chaplains seems designed for his grandfather. Tom was reared in a rectory, with his grandfather, an Episcopalian priest, as father-substitute. Here he pictures the "good" chaplain, who confronts the warden about prison conditions, in contrast to the accommodating "Reverend." This scene is pure slapstick, as Tom scribbled in the margin of the script: "Preposterous situation, completely out of key with rest of play. . . ." Is *Not About Nightingales* in fact a tragedy? Does Jim survive? Perhaps the answer is in the siren-like name of the passing pleasure boat, the *Lorelei*. Williams has written the first of his ambiguous endings.

By the end of 1938, as the harangues about money increased at home, Tom's final hope was to get to New York. He wrote on the back of his script the names of eleven Broadway producers and "three wealthy non-professionals." At the last minute he chose to go to New Orleans instead, where the Writers' Project was still operating. En route he mailed a packet of plays to a Group Theatre contest for writers under twenty-five. Tom was twenty-seven, but felt justified in dropping the three years he had worked in the factory as "lost time." He sent four one-acts under the title *American Blues,* as well as *Fugitive Kind* and *Not About Nightingales,* for the first time signing himself "Tennessee Williams." In 1939, just before his twenty-eighth birthday, he received the wire that the Group Theatre had created a special award of one hundred dollars for his first three sketches in *American Blues.* Molly Day Thacher, wife of Elia Kazan, wrote that she would write him later about *Not About Nightingales.* It was she who brought Tom to the attention of agent Audrey Wood, who launched his Broadway career and changed his life.

Why was this play never produced? In 1939 a Broadway agent may have found a play with murder, violent death, a sympathetic Black character, a drag queen, and syphilis difficult to market. Times were changing. Coming war brought full employment, ending the Depression. With the advent of Joseph McCarthy in the Senate and the "red scare," revolutionary plays were suspect. The rising power of the House Un-American Activities Committee which ruined the careers of many theatre people, including the actor John Garfield, put an end to the idealistic Federal Theatre Project, branding it as Communist.

Williams himself was moving towards a different sort of play, psychological rather than sociological, although his writing would always attack injustice and defend society's misfits. If *Not About Nightingales* is to some extent a period piece, derivative in some ways, unique in others, it merits consideration as an apprentice play by America's master playwright, on the way to finding his own distinctive voice.

—Allean Hale
January, 1998

Not About Nightingales was given its world premier on March 5, 1998, at the Royal National Theatre, London, England. *Nightingales* was directed by Trevor Nunn; set design was by Richard Hoover; costume design by Fizz Jones; lighting by Chris Parry, and sound by Christopher Shutt. Production Manager was Diane Willmott and Stage Manager was Courtney Bryant. The cast, in order of appearance, was as follows:

EVA CRANE	SHERRI PARKER LEE
MRS. BRISTOL	SANDRA DICKINSON
JIM ALLISON (CANARY JIM)	FINBAR LYNCH
BOSS WHALEN, *the warden*	CORIN REDGRAVE
JACK BRISTOL (SAILOR JACK)	RICHARD LEAF
SCHULTZ, *a guard*	RICHARD ZIMAN
BUTCH O'FALLON	JAMES BLACK
THE QUEEN	JUKE AKUWUDIKE
JOE	ALEX GIANNINI
MCBURNEY, *a guard*	CRAIG PINDER
OLLIE	DION GRAHAM
SWIFTY	MARK DEXTER
GOLDIE, *an apparition*	SANDRA DICKINSON
SHAPIRO	JOEL LEFFERT
MEX	CHICO ANDRADE
CHAPLAIN	TOM HODGKINS
REVEREND HOOKER	NOBLE SHROPSHIRE
GUARDS, CONVICTS, TROOPERS	MARK HEENEHAN,
	RICHARD LEAF,
	DANIEL STEWART,
	NOBLE SHROPSHIRE

PRODUCTION NOTE

Because they illustrate the young Williams' experimentation, two excerpts from an earlier variant of the play called *Hell, an Expressionistic Drama* are included in our 1938 script. "Butch Has a Dream," added as Episode Seven, projects fantasy into a starkly real drama. "Hell—An Expressionistic Interlude," is inserted as Episode Ten because it enacts visibly what the playwright merely summarized in his final draft and suggests both his staging innovations and his musicality. Both episodes demonstrate Williams' early tendency to move from the real to the surreal. (Williams may have left the "Strikers' Chant" out of the final playscript because the refrain "Turn up the heat" too directly anticipates the play's climax.) A third addition optional in performance is the "Flash forward to end of play" at the end of the "Opening" where Eva is shown clutching Jim's shoes.

The playwright's instructions of "Theme Up" and "Fade Out" in the manuscript suggest that he may have intended theme music for each episode. When specific music is indicated, we have included it in the script.

—A. H.

This play is dedicated to the memory
of Clarence Darrow, The Great Defender,
whose mental frontiers were the
four corners of the sky.

OPENING

The action takes place in a large American prison during the summer of 1938. The conditions which the play presents are those of no particular prison but a composite picture of many.

LOUD-SPEAKER: "Yeah, this is the Lorelei excursion steamer, All-day trip around Sandy Point. Leave 8 A.M., return at Midnight. Sight-seeing, dancing, entertainment with Lorelei Lou and her eight Lorelights! Got your ticket, lady? Got your ticket? Okay, that's all. We're shoving off now. Now we're leaving the boat dock, folks. We're out in the harbor. Magnificent skyline of the city against the early morning sunlight. It's still a little misty around the tops of the big towers downtown. Hear those bells ringing? That's St. Patrick's Cathedral. Finest chimes in America. It's eight o'clock sharp. Sun's bright as a dollar, swell day, bright, warm, makes you mighty proud to be alive, yes, Ma'am! There it is! You can see it now, folks. That's the Island. Sort of misty still. See them big stone walls. Dynamite-proof, escape-proof! Thirty-five hundred men in there, folks, and lots of 'em 'll never get out! Boy, oh, boy, I wonder how it feels t' be locked up in a place like that till doomsday? Oh, oh!! There goes the band, folks! Dancing on the Upper Deck! Dancing, folks! Lorelei Lou and her eight Lorelights! Dancing on the Upper Deck—dancing! —Dancing! —Dancing. . . [*Fade.*]

[*Flash forward to end of play. Light fades except for a spot on Eva, clutching Jim's shoes.*]

LOUD-SPEAKER: Aw, there it is! You can see it now, folks. That's the Island! Sort of misty tonight. You'd see it better if there was a moon. Those walls are dynamite-proof, escape-proof—Thirty-five hundred men in there—some won't get out till Doomsday. —There's the band! —Dancing on the Upper

Deck, folks! Lorelei Lou and her eight Lorelights! Dancing—dancing—dancing. . . [*Fade.*]

[*Music comes up. The shoes fall from Eva's hands, and she covers her face.*]

BLACKOUT

ACT ONE

Announcer: "Miss Crane Applies for a Job"

A spot lights the bench outside the Warden's office where Mrs. Bristol is sitting. Mrs. B is a worn matron in black, holding a napkin-covered basket on her lap. Eva enters the spot from the right and sits on the bench, nervously. She grips her pocketbook tensely and stares straight ahead.

MRS. B: Your hat!

EVA: My hat?

MRS. B: Yes, look!

EVA: Oh, dear!

MRS. B: Here.

EVA: Thanks!

[*Mrs. Bristol removes a spot from Eva's hat with tissue paper from her basket.*]

MRS. B: It's those pigeons, the little rascals!

EVA: Yes, they're much too casual about such things.

MRS. B: It's such a nice hat, too.

EVA: Oh, it's quite old. [*She puts the hat back on and drops her purse.*]

3

MRS. B: You're nervous.

EVA: So nervous I could scream!

MRS. B: Is it your husband?

EVA: Who?

MRS. B: That you're coming to see about?

EVA: Oh, no. No I'm coming to see about a job.

MRS. B: A job? Here?

EVA: Yes, here. I've heard there's a vacancy.

MRS. B: But wouldn't you find it an awfully depressing sort of place to work in?

EVA: I don't think so. It's not an ordinary prison.

MRS. B: Isn't it?

EVA: No, it's supposed to be a model institution.

MRS. B: A model institution!

EVA: Yes, everything's done scientifically they say. They've got experts—in psychology and sociology and things like that, you know!

MRS. B: Well!

EVA: The old idea used to be punishment of crime but nowadays it's—social rehabilitation!

MRS. B: Now just imagine! How did you come to know?

EVA: I read all about it in the *Sunday Supplement*!

[*Jim passes across the spot.*]

EVA [*jumping up*]: May I see the Warden?

JIM: Sorry. He's not back yet. [*He crosses into the door of the office.*]

EVA: Oh.

MRS. B: I've got a son in here. He used to be a sailor. Jack's his name.

EVA: A sailor?

MRS. B: Yes, he was one of Uncle Sam's Navy-boys. Till he got in trouble with some kind of woman.

EVA: What a shame!

MRS. B: Yes, wasn't it though—the common slut! —Excuse me but that's what she was. My Scott! [*She clutches her bosom.*]

EVA: What?

MRS. B: I've got the most awful palpitations!

EVA [*jumping up*]: You're sick? Let me get you some water!

MRS. B: No, thanks, dear. I'll just take one of my phenobarbital tablets, and I'll be all right in a jiffy. [*Stage business.*] I've been under such a strain lately with Jack on my mind all the time.

EVA: You shouldn't be worried. My landlady's brother-in-law is one of the guards—it was through him that I heard about this vacancy—and he says they have less serious trouble here than any penitentiary in the country. Mr. Whalen, the Warden, is very highly respected.

MRS. B: Well, I do hope you're right for Jack's sake. But I haven't gotten much comfort out of his letters. Especially the last one. It was that one which upset me so. It wasn't at all like those long marvelous letters that he used to write me when he was at sea. It was scribbled in such a bad hand and—well—it sounded sort of—*feverish* to me! —What is Klondike?

EVA: Klondike? Part of Alaska!

MRS. B: That's what I thought. But in Jack's letter he said he'd been sent down there and it was as hot as—well, I won't say it!

EVA: Possibly it's one of those colonization schemes.

MRS. B: No, I don't think so. In fact I'm positive it isn't. He said they wouldn't let him write me about it if they knew, so he was sneakin' the letter out by one of the boys.

EVA: How long does he have to stay here?

MRS. B: Five years!

EVA: Oh, that's not so long.

MRS. B: It seems like forever to me.

EVA: He'll probably come out a better and stronger boy than before he went in.

MRS. B: Oh no. They couldn't make a better and stronger boy than Jack was. I don't understand all about it, but I know one thing—whatever happened it wasn't my boy's fault! —And that's what I'm going to say to the Warden soon as I get in to see him—I've been waiting here two days—he never has time!

EVA [rising]: I can't stand waiting. It makes me too nervous. I'm going right in and make that young fellow tell me when Mr. Whalen will be here.

MRS. B: Yes, do! Tell him how long I've been waiting! And ask him if Jack—

[Eva has already entered office—Mrs. B sinks slowly down, clutching her bosom.]

Oh, dear. . .

[The spot moves from the bench to the interior of the office.]

EVA [at the door]: I beg your pardon.

JIM [giving her a long look]: For what?

EVA: For intruding like this. But I couldn't sit still any longer. When can I see Mr. Whalen?

JIM: What about?

EVA: A job.

[*Jim is filing papers in a cabinet. He continues all the while.*]

JIM: He's out right now. Inspecting the grounds.

EVA: Oh. Will it take him long?

JIM: That depends on how much grounds he feels like inspecting.

EVA: Oh.

JIM: Sometimes inspecting the grounds doesn't mean inspecting the grounds. [*He gives her a brief smile.*]

EVA: Doesn't it?

JIM: No. [*He crumples a paper.*] Sometimes it's an idiomatic expression for having a couple of beers in the back room at Tony's which is a sort of unofficial clubhouse for the prison staff —Would you like to sit down?

EVA: About how long do you suppose I'd have to wait?

JIM: It's a hot afternoon. He might do a lot of ground-inspection and then again he might not. His actions are pretty unpredictable. That's a good word.

EVA: What?

JIM: Unpredictable. Anything with five syllables is a good word.

EVA: You like long words?

JIM: They're my stock-in-trade. I'm supposed to use a lot of
'em to impress you with my erudition. There's another one
right there!

EVA: Erudition?

JIM: Yes, only four but it's unusual. I get 'em all out of this
big book.

EVA: Dictionary?

JIM: *Webster's Unabridged.* [*He slams the file cabinet shut
and leans against it.*] Y'see I'm one of the exhibition pieces.

EVA: Are you really?

JIM: I'm supposed to tell you that when I came in here I was
just an ordinary grifter. But look at me now. I'm reading
Spengler's *Decline of the West* and I'm editor of the prison
monthly. Ask me what is an archaeopteryx.

EVA: What is it?

JIM: An extinct species of reptile-bird. Here's our latest issue.

EVA [*more and more confused*]: Of—what?

JIM: *The Archaeopteryx.* Our monthly publication.

EVA: Why do you call it that?

JIM: It sounds impressive. Do you know what an amaranth is?

EVA: No. What is it?

JIM: A flower that never dies. [*He lifts a book.*] I came across it in here. One of the classical poets compares it to love. What's your opinion of that.

EVA: Well, I—what's yours?

JIM: I wouldn't know. I started my present career at the age of sixteen.

EVA: That early.

JIM: Yes, the usual case of bad influences. And at that age of course—love is something you dream about and blush when you look at yourself in the mirror next morning! [*He laughs. Eva looks away in slight confusion.*] Say, d'you know that song?

EVA: What song?

JIM [*giving a sour imitation*]: "Ah, tis love and love alone the world is seeking!" A guy sang it in chapel last night—Is that on the level?

EVA: Well, I—not exactly.

JIM: You're inclined to admit a few qualifications?

EVA: Yes. For instance what I'm seeking is a job. And a new pair of stockings.

JIM: Those look good to me.

EVA: They're worn to shreds!

JIM: Well, perhaps I'm prejudiced.

[*Eva clears her throat. Jim clears his.*]

EVA [*picking up the newspaper*]: "Prison: the door to Opportunity!"

JIM: Yes, that's one of my best editorials. It's been reproduced all over the country—I got ten years of copper for writing that.

EVA: Copper?

JIM: Not what they make pennies out of. In here copper means good time. Time off your sentence for good behavior. I've got about ten years of copper stashed away in the files and most of it's for extolling the inspirational quality of prison life—

[*Mrs. Bristol enters timidly, clutching her basket.*]

JIM: Hello.

MRS. B: How do you do. Is Mr. Whalen in yet?

JIM: No, he's still out inspecting the grounds.

MRS. B: Oh, I do so want to see him this afternoon. I'm—I'm Jack Bristol's mother.

JIM: Sailor Jack?

MRS. B [*advancing a few steps*]: Yes—yes! You—know him?

11

JIM: Slightly.

MRS. B [*struggling to speak*]: How is my boy?

JIM: Sorry. I'm not allowed to give out information.

MRS. B: Oh.

JIM: You'd better talk to Mr. Whalen tomorrow morning.

MRS. B: What time, please?

JIM: Ten o'clock.

MRS. B: Ten o'clock. Could you give him these now? [*She places the basket carefully on the table.*] I'm afraid they'll get stale if they're kept any longer. They're for my boy. [*She turns slowly and goes out.*]

EVA: Couldn't you tell her something to relieve her mind?

JIM: Not about Sailor Jack!

EVA: Why not?

JIM: He's gone—stir bugs.

EVA: You mean?

JIM [*touching his forehead*]: Cracked up in here. It's sort of an occupational disease among convicts.

EVA: But they said in the *Sunday Supplement*—

JIM: I know. They interviewed me and the Warden.

EVA: You didn't tell them the truth?

JIM: What is it that Plato said about truth? Truth is—truth is— Funny I can't remember! Was it the *Sunday Supplement* that gave you the idea of getting a job in here?

EVA: That and my landlady. Her brother-in-law is Mr. McBurney, one of the prison guards.

JIM: Mac's a pretty good screw.

EVA: What?

JIM: That means a guard in here. Here's one of our sample menus. It shows what a connie gets to eat every day. You can see that it compares quite favorably with the bill-of-fare at any well-known boarding school. Everything's done scientifically here. We have an expert dietitian. Weighs everything by calories. Units of body heat— Hello, Mr. Whalen!

[*Whalen enters. He is a powerful man, rather stout, but with coarse good looks.*]

WARDEN: Hello, hello there! [*He removes his coat and tosses it to Jim.*] Breezy day, hot breezy day! [*He winks at Jim, then belches.*] Too much ground-inspection! [*He loosens his collar and tie.*] Excuse me, lady, I'm going to do a striptease! Yep, it's a mighty wind—feels like it comes out of an oven! Reminds me of those— [*He wipes his forehead.*] —those beautiful golden-brown biscuits my mother used to bake! What's this? [*He removes the cover from the basket.*] Speak of biscuits and what turns up but a nice batch of homemade cookies! Have one, young lady—Jimmy boy!

[Jim takes two.]

Uh-h, you've got an awful big paw, Jimmy! [*He laughs.*] Show the new Arky-what's-it to Miss *Daily News*—or is it the *Morning Star*? Have a chair! I'll be right with you— [*He vanishes for a moment into the inner room.*] Sweat, sweat, sweat's all I do these hot breezy days!

JIM [*sotto voce*]: He thinks you're a newspaper woman.

WARDEN [*emerging*]: Turn on that fan. Well, now, let's see—

EVA: To begin with I'm not—

WARDEN: You've probably come here to question me about that ex-convict's story in that damned yellow sheet down there in Wilkes County— That stuff about getting pellagra in here— Jimmy, hand me that sample menu!

JIM: She's not a reporter.

WARDEN: Aw. —What *is* your business, young lady?

EVA [*in breathless haste*]: I understand that there's a vacancy here. Mr. McBurney, my landlady's brother-in-law, told her that you were needing a new stenographer, and I'm sure that I can qualify for the position. I'm a college graduate, Mr. Whalen. I've had three years of business experience—references with me—but, oh—I've—I've had such abominable luck these last six months—the last place I worked—the business recession set in—they had to cut down on their salesforce—they gave me a wonderful letter—I've got it with me— [*She opens her purse and spills its contents on the floor.*] Oh, goodness! I've—broken my glasses!

WARDEN [*coldly*]: Yeah?

EVA [*rising slowly*]: Could you give me a job? —Please, I'm—terribly nervous, I—if I don't get a job soon I'll—

WARDEN: What? Go off the deep end?

EVA: Yes, something like that! [*She smiles desperately.*]

WARDEN: Well, Miss—uh—

EVA [*eagerly*]: Crane! Eva Crane!

WARDEN: They call that window the "Quick Way Out"! It's the only one in the house without bars. I don't need bars. It's right over the bay. So if it's suicide you got in mind that window is at your disposal. No, Miss Crane. Next time you apply for a job don't pull a sob story. What your business executive is interested in is your potential value, not your—your personal misfortunes! [*He takes a cigar.*]

EVA [*turning away*]: I see. Then I—

WARDEN: Hold on a minute.

EVA: Yes?

WARDEN [*biting and spitting out the end of the cigar*]: There's just one prerequisite for a job in this office. Jimmy will explain that to you.

EVA [*turning to Jim*]: Yes?

JIM: The ability to keep your mouth shut except when you're given specific instructions to speak!

WARDEN: Think you could do that?

EVA: Yes.

JIM: The motorboat leaves the dock at seven forty-five in the morning.

EVA: Thanks—Yes, *thanks!* [*She turns quickly and goes out, blind with joy.*]

WARDEN: What do you think of her, Jimmy boy? Okay, huh?

JIM: Yes, Sir.

WARDEN: Yes, Siree! Dizzy as hell— But she's got a shape on her that would knock the bricks out of a Federal Pen! [*He erupts in sudden booming laughter.*]

DIM OUT

EPISODE TWO

Announcer: *"Sailor Jack."*

Musical theme up: *"Auprès de ma Blonde."* Fade.

There is a spot on a cell. Electric lights from the corridor throw the shadow of bars across floor. The cell is empty except for the figure of Sailor Jack, slumped on a stool with the shadow of bars thrown across him. His face has the vacant look of the schizophrenic, and he is mumbling inaudibly to himself. His voice rises—

SAILOR JACK: Where? Port Said! —And not one of 'em but woulda done it 'emselves if they'd 'ad ha'f a chance. [*He begins to sing hoarsely.*]

> *Auprès de ma blonde*
> *Il fait bon, fait bon, fait bon!*
> *Auprès de ma blonde*
> *qu'il fait bon dormir!*

No chance for advancement, huh? What would you say if I told you that I was Admiral of the whole bitchin' navy? [*He laughs.*]

> *Je donnerai Versailles,*
> *Paris et Saint Denis—*

[*Sounds are heard: a shrill whistle in hall and the shuffle of feet: the door of the cell clangs open and Joe, Butch, and the Queen enter.*]

SCHULTZ: Lights out in five minutes.

BUTCH: Ahh, yuh fruit, go toot yuh goddam horn outa here. Mus' think they runnin' a stinkin' sweatshop, this workin' overtime stuff. Git yuh task done or come back after supper. Goddam machine got stuck. Delib'rate sabotage, he calls it. I'd like to sabotage his guts. [*To Queen*.]: What happened to you this mornin'?

QUEEN [*in a high tenor voice*]: I got an awful pain in the back of my neck and flipped out. When I come to I was in the hospital. They was stickin' a needle in my arm— Say! What does plus four mean?

JOE: Christ! It means—

BUTCH: Pocket yuh marbles!

QUEEN: Naw. Is it bad?

JOE: We're in swell sassiety, Butch. A lunatic an' a case of the syph!

QUEEN: The syph?

[*A whistle is heard: the lights dim in the corridor.*]

QUEEN: Naw! [*He tries to laugh.*] It don't mean that!

SAILOR: *Auprès de ma blonde*
        Il fait bon, fait bon, fait bon!
        Auprès de ma blonde—

SCHULTZ: Cut the cackle in there! It's after lights.

BUTCH: God damn it, can't you see he's blown his top?

JOE: Yeah, get him out of here!

SCHULTZ: He's putting on an act.

SAILOR: *Je donnerai Versailles,*
Paris et Saint Denis—

SCHULTZ: You take another trip to Klondike, Sailor, it won't be on a round-trip ticket!

BUTCH: It's Klondike that got him like this. He's been ravin' ever since you brung him upstairs. You must've cooked the brains out of him down there, Schultz.

SAILOR: *La Tour d'Eiffel aussi!*

SCHULTZ [*rapping the bars*]: Dummy up, the lot of you! One more squawk an' I'll call the strong-arm squad!

QUEEN: Mr. Schultz!

SCHULTZ: Yeah?

QUEEN: What does plus four mean?

[*Schultz laughs and moves off.*]

BUTCH: If I wasn't scared of losin' all my copper I'd reach through and grab that bastard. I'd rattle them pea-pod brains of his 'n roll 'em out on the floor like a pair of dice. The trouble is in here you gotta pick your man. If I rubbed out a screw I'd never git a chance at the boss. —What time is it?

JOE: Ten-thirty.

BUTCH: Mac comes on duty now.

JOE: You think he'll take the Sailor out?

BUTCH: I'll tell him to.

QUEEN: Naw. It's nothin' that serious or they woulda kept me in the hospital. It's just indigestion. That's what I told 'em, I said the food is no good. It don't set good on my stomach. Spaghetti, spaghetti, spaghetti! I said I'm sicka spaghetti!

SAILOR: *Auprès de ma blonde*
Il fait bon, fait bon, fait bon!
Auprès de ma blonde
qu'il fait bon dormir!

[*Butch clips him with a fist.*]

JOE: What did you do that for?

BUTCH: You wanta tangle with the strong-arm squadron on account of him?

[*A whistle is heard: doors clang.*]

They're changin' now. [*He goes to the bars.*] Who's 'at? McBurney?

MAC: What do you want, Butch?

BUTCH: For Chrissakes git this kid outta here.

MAC: Which kid?

BUTCH: Sailor Jack. He's been stir-bugs since they brung him upstairs a week ago Tuesday.

MAC [*at the door*]: What's he doing?

BUTCH: He's out right now. I had to conk him one.

MAC: What did they tell you about roughin' up the boys?

BUTCH: Roughin'? ME? Lissen! —Ask Joe, ask anybody, ask the Canary—the kid had blown his top—Schultz was gonna call the strong-arm squad an' have us all thrown in Klondike cause he wouldn't quit singin' them dirty French songs! Ain't that right, Joe?

JOE: Sure, Mac.

[*Whistle.*]

MAC: Where's his stuff?

BUTCH: Here. I got it tied up nice.

MAC: Well, it's no put-in of mine. He should've done his task in the shop.

BUTCH: He done his task pretty good.

JOE: That boy worked hard.

MAC: Not hard enough to suit the Boss.

[*Enter guards.*]

Awright, git him outta here. Put him in isolation tonight an' have him looked after tomorrow.

QUEEN: Mr. McBurney, what does plus four mean? Mr. McBurney—

[*Mac goes out with guards carrying Sailor. Bird calls are heard in the hall.*]

VOICE [*in hall*]: Goodnight, Mac.

MAC: G'night, Jim.

BUTCH: Who's 'at? Allison?

JOE: Yeah. It's the Canary.

SAILOR [*from down the hall*]: *"Auprès de ma blonde Il fait bon, fait bon, fait bon!"*

[*The sound fades.*]

BUTCH: Hey, Canary! Allison!

[*The spot shifts to include Allison's cell.*]

JIM: What do you want, Butch? [*He is shown removing his shirt and shoes.*]

BUTCH: Next time you're in a huddle with the boss tell him the Angels in Hall C have put another black mark on his name for Sailor Jack.

JIM: I'll tell him that.

BUTCH: Tell him some day we're going to appoint a special committee of one to come down there an' settle up the score. —You hear me, Stool?

JIM: I hear you.

BUTCH: Just think—I used to be cell-mates with him. I lie awake at night regrettin' all the times I had a chance to split his guts—but didn't!

JOE: Why didn'tcha?

BUTCH: That was before he started workin' for the boss. But now he's number three on the Angel's Records. First Whalen, then Schultz, and then the Stool! You hear that, Stool?

JIM: Yes, I hear you, Butch. [*He rolls and lights a cigarette.*]

BUTCH: That's good. I'm glad you do.

JIM: I know you're glad.

JOE: What's he say?

BUTCH: He says he knows I'm glad.

JOE: He oughta know. Wonder he don't go stir-bugs, too. Nobody have nothin' to do with him but Ollie.

BUTCH: He'll blow his top sometime, if I don't git him first. You hear that, Stool? I said you'll blow your top sometime like Sailor Jack—I'm lookin' forward to it.

JOE: What's he say?

BUTCH: Nothin'. He's smokin' in there.

JOE: We oughta tip 'em off.

BUTCH: Naw, I never ratted on nobody. Not even that Stool.

QUEEN: Allison! Hey! Jim! What does plus four mean?

JIM: Who's got plus four?

QUEEN: I have. What does it mean, Jim?

JIM: It means your physical condition is four points above perfect.

QUEEN [*relieved*]: Aw. These bastards had me worried.

BUTCH [*climbing on a stool by the window*]: Foghorns. It's thick as soup outside— Lissen!

JOE: What?

BUTCH: Excursion steamer.

JOE: Which one?

BUTCH: The Lorelei.

JOE: Lookit them lights on her, will yuh. Red, white, green, yellow!

BUTCH: Hear that orchester?

JOE: What're they playin'?

BUTCH: "Roses a Picardy!"

JOE: That's an old one.

BUTCH: It come up the year I got sent up. Why, I remember dancin' to that piece. At the Princess Ballroom. With Goldie. She requested that number ev'ry time I took her out on the floor. We danced there the night they pinched me. On the way out—right at the turn-stile—them six bulls met me—six of 'em—that's how many it took—they had the wagon waitin' at the curb.

JOE: Last time it was four bulls. You're gettin' less conservative, Butch.

BUTCH: "Roses a Picardy." I'd like to dance that number one more time. With Goldie.

JOE: Maybe it was her that put the finger on you.

BUTCH: Naw. Not Goldie. I bet that girl's still holdin' the torch for me.

JOE: Keep your illusions, Butch, if they're a comfort to yuh. But I bet if Goldie was still holdin' all the torches that she's held before an' after you got put in the stir she'd throw more light across the water than a third-alarm fire!

QUEEN: Where's my manicure set?

BUTCH: I wonder if a guy is any good at sixty?

JOE: What do you mean?

BUTCH: You know. With women.

JOE: I guess it depends on the guy.

BUTCH: I'll still be good. But twenty years is a lot of time to wait.

QUEEN: Has anybody seen my manicure set?

BUTCH: You know there's a window in Boss Whalen's office from which a guy could jump right into the Bay.

JOE: Yeah. The Quick Way Out.

BUTCH: I was thinkin' that it would be a good way to kill two birds with a stone. Rub him out an' jump through that window for the getaway. Providin' you could swim. But me I can't swim a goddam stroke. I wish that I'd learned how before I come in here.

JOE: Wouldn't do you no good. Nobody's ever swum it yet.

BUTCH: I'd like to try. —They say some people swim instinctive like a duck.

JOE: You'd take a chance on that?

BUTCH: Naw. I'm scared a water.

QUEEN [excitedly]: I put it here last night. Butch, did you see it?

BUTCH: What?

QUEEN: My manicure set.

BUTCH: It's gone out wit' the slop-bucket.

QUEEN: What did you do that for?

BUTCH: It stunk up the place. Smelt like rotten bananas—What's this on Sailor Jack's bunk?

JOE: A package a letters from his ole lady.

BUTCH: Aw.

JOE: She said she was comin' from Wisconsin to see him in the last one.

QUEEN: All my life I've been persecuted by people because I'm refined.

BUTCH: Somebody oughta told her how the Sailor is.

JOE: Well, she'll find out.

QUEEN: Because I'm sensitive I been persecuted all my life!

BUTCH: Yeah, she'll find out.

QUEEN: Sometimes I wish I was dead. Oh, Lord, Lord, Lord! I wish I was dead!

[*Musical theme up. Fade.*]

BLACKOUT

EPISODE THREE

A spot comes up on the Warden's office. He's looking at a racing form-sheet when Eva Crane, his secretary, enters.

WARDEN [*lifting the phone and dialing*]: How's the track, Bert? Fast? Okay. I want twenty bucks on Windy Blue to show. [*He hangs up.*] Anybody outside?

EVA: Yes. That woman.

WARDEN: What woman?

EVA: The one from Wisconsin. She's still waiting—

WARDEN: I told you I— [*Sailor Jack's mother has quietly entered. She carries a neatly wrapped bundle in brown paper—she smiles diffidently at the Warden.*]

MRS. B: I beg your pardon, I—I took the liberty of coming in. I hope you won't mind. You see I'm Jack Bristol's mother and I've been wanting to have a talk with you so long about—about my boy!

WARDEN: Set down. I'm pretty short on time.

MRS. B: I won't take much. To begin with, Mr. Whalen, I never felt the jury did exactly right in giving Jack three years. But that's done now. I've got to look to the future.

WARDEN: Yes, the future—that's right.

MRS. B: I haven't heard from Jack lately. He'd been writing me once a week till just lately.

WARDEN: Lots of boys get careless about their correspondence.

MRS. B: For two years not a week passed without a letter. Then suddenly just a month ago they stopped coming. Naturally I felt rather anxious.

WARDEN: Jim!

JIM: Yes, sir?

WARDEN: Check on a boy named Bristol.

MRS. B: Thank you, I—I came all the way from Wisconsin.

WARDEN: Long trip, huh? Wisconsin's where they make all that fine cheese.

MRS. B: Yes, we're very proud of our dairy products up there. [*She looks anxiously after Jim who has gone slowly to the file-case as though stalling for time.*]

WARDEN: They manufacture the best cheese this side of Switzerland. Yes, Siree!

MRS. B: Jack's last letter was strange. I—I have it with me. It's not at all like Jack. He wasn't transferred to any other prison, was he? Because he kept complaining all through his letter about how terribly hot it was in a place called Klondike. His penmanship has always been quite irregular but this was so bad I could scarcely read it at all—I thought possibly he wasn't well when he wrote it—feverish, you know—he's very subject to colds especially this time of year. I—I brought this wool comforter with me. For Jack. I know it's not easy, Mr. Whalen, to

29

make exceptions in an institution like this. But in Jack's case where there are so many, *many* considerations—so much that I regret *myself* when I look back at things— Mistakes that I made—

WARDEN: Mistakes, yes, we all make mistakes.

MRS. B: Such *grave* mistakes, Mr. Whalen. Our household was not an altogether happy one, you see. Jack's father—well, he was a Methodist minister and his views naturally differed quite a bit from most young boys'—

WARDEN [*with a cynical smile.*]: A preacher's son?

MRS. B: Yes! But there was a disagreement among the congregation not long ago and my husband was forced to retire.

WARDEN [*impatiently*]: I see. I'm very busy, I— [*To Jim.*]: Have you found that card?

JIM [*stalling*]: Not yet.

MRS. B: He was so—so uncompromising, even with poor Jack. So Jack left home. Of course it was against my wishes but— [*She opens her bag and produces sheaf of letters.*] Oh, those long marvelous letters that he wrote! If you would only read them you'd see for yourself what an exceptional boy Jack was. Port Said, Marseilles, Cairo, Shanghai, Bombay! "Oh, mother, it's so big, so terribly, terribly big," he kept on writing. As though he'd tried to squeeze it in his heart until the bigness of it made this heart crack open! Look! These envelopes! You see they're packed so full that he could hardly close them! Pictures of places, too! Elephants in India. They're used like packhorses, he said, for common labor. Little Chinese junkets have square sails. They scoot about like dragonflies on top of the water. The bay at Rangoon. Here's where the sun comes up like thunder, he wrote on the back of this one! Kipling, you know— I wrote him constantly—"Jack, there's no advancement in it. A sailor's always a sailor. Get out of it, son. Get into the Civil Service!" He wrote me back—"I kept the middle watch last night. You see more stars down here than in the northern water. The Southern Cross is right above me now, but won't be long—because our course is changing—" I stopped opposing then, I thought that anything he loved as much as that would surely keep him safe. And then he didn't write a while—until this came. I still can't understand it! He mentioned a girl— He said it wasn't his fault, I know that it wasn't— If I could convince you of that—!

WARDEN: It's no use ma'am! You might as well be talking to the moon. He's had his chance.

MRS. B: But in Jack's case—!

WARDEN: I know, I know. I've heard all that before. Jim, have you found that card?

JIM [*coming slowly forward with a card from files*]: You'd better look at it yourself.

WARDEN: Read it, read it! We running a social service bureau?

[*Jim looks uncertainly at Mrs. Bristol who raises a clenched hand to her breast.*]

MRS. B [*softly*]: If anything's gone wrong I'd like to know.

JIM [*reading huskily*]: "Jack Bristol. Larceny. Convicted May,

1936. Sentenced three years." [*Looks up.*] He slacked his work. Spent three days in Klondike.

WARDEN [*sharply*]: Is that on the card?

JIM: No, but I wanted to explain to this lady what happened.

MRS. B: [*rising slowly*]: What happened?

JIM: You see, ma'am—

WARDEN [*sharply*]: Read what's on the card, that's all!

JIM: "Came up before the lunacy commission, May 1938, transferred to the psychopathic ward. Violent. Delusions. Prognosis—Dementia Praecox"—

[*Pause.*]

MRS. B: That isn't—Jack—my boy!

WARDEN: Now see here—I— [*He motions to Jim to get her out.*] I know how you feel about this. I got all the sympathy in the world for you women that come in here, but this is a penal institution and we simply can't be taking time out from our routine business for things like this.

MRS. B: My boy, Jack, my boy! Not what you said! Anything but that! Say he's dead, say you killed him, killed him! But don't tell me that. I know, I know. I know how it was in here. He wrote me letters. The food not decent. I tried to send him food—he didn't get it—no, even that you took from him. That place you sent him three days. Klondike. I know—You tortured him there, that's what you did, you tortured him until you drove him— [*She turns slowly to Jim.*] —Crazy? Is that what you said? —Oh, my precious Jesus, oh, my God! [*She breaks down, sobbing wildly.*]

WARDEN: Get that woman out!

[*Jim assists her to the door.*]

Whew! [*He lights a cigar and picks up the form-sheet.*]

BLACKOUT

Announcer: "Conversations at Midnight!"

The spot lights the two cells with a partition between. Ollie kneels praying by his bunk. Butch lounges, covertly smoking, on a bench along the wall. The others sit on their bunks.

OLLIE [*in an audible whisper*]: Oh, Lawd, de proteckter an preserbation ob all, remebuh dis nigguh. Remebuh his wife Susie an his six chillun, Rachel, Rebekah, Solomon, Moses, Ecclesiastics an' Deuteronomy Jackson. You look out fo' dem while Ise in jail. An ah'd git out fo de cole weathuh sets in cause Susie's gonna have another baby, Lawd, an' she can't git aroun't' gatherin' kindlin' wood. God bless my ole woman an' daddy an' Presiden' Roosevelt an' de W.P.A.* in Jesus Chris' name—Amen. [*He rises stiffly.*]

BUTCH [*grinning*]: Hey, Ollie, yuh better have 'em reverse the charges on that one!

OLLIE: It don' cos' nothin'.

BUTCH: It ain't worth nothin'.

OLLIE: De Lawd remembuhs who remembuhs Him.

BUTCH: Hawshit!

[*Ollie sits dejectedly on the edge of his bunk. There are derisive whistles and bird-calls in the hall as Jim enters.*]

---

*The Works Progress Administration (W.P.A.) was a Depression era agency created by President Franklin D. Roosevelt and the United States Congress in 1935 to give employment to persons on the relief rolls.

JIM: Whatsamatter, Ollie?

OLLIE [*jerking his thumb at Butch's cell*]: He says there ain't no God.

JIM: How's he know?

OLLIE: That's what I say.

[*Jim removes his shirt and swabs sweat off his face and chest with it, then pitches it into the corner. He picks up a naked art magazine and fans himself with it.*]

OLLIE: You think they is, don't you, Jim?

JIM: Somebody upstairs? —I dunno. I guess I'm what they call an agnostic.

OLLIE: You mean a Piscopalian?

JIM: Yeah. Rub my back for me, Ollie. I'm tired.

OLLIE: Awright. Liniment aw bacon grease?

JIM: Gimme the liniment.

BUTCH: Haven't you started seein' 'em yet, Canary?

JIM [*as Ollie starts to rub*]: Gawd, it burns good.

BUTCH: Them little blue devils, they're the first symptom.

JIM: It makes the air feel cool.

BUTCH: They crawl in through the bars an' sit on the end of yuh bunk an' make faces at yuh.

JIM: Rub harder on the left shoulder.

BUTCH: Yuh'd better start sleepin' with one eye open, Canary. Can yuh do that?

JIM: Never tried it, Butch. —Ah, that's good.

BUTCH: Well, yuh better, cause if they catch you off guard, Canary, they'll climb down yuh throat an' tie knots in yuh gizzard! [*He laughs delightedly at the prospect.*]

JIM: That's good, ah that's—swell.

OLLIE: How'd you get them purple scars, Jim?

JIM: From Dr. Jones.

OLLIE: Who's Dr. Jones?

BUTCH: Dr. Jones is the guy that gave Canary his singin' lessons! Remembuh when I found out that you'd grown feathers?

JIM [*to Ollie*]: That's enough. Thanks. [*He produces cigarettes.*] Have one?

OLLIE: Thanks, Jim.

BUTCH: It's lucky for you that I was interrupted—or you'd be readin' books witcha fingers instead of yer eyes! It's listed on th' record as unfinished business, to be took care of at some future date—I figure that ev'ry dog has his day an' mine's comin' pretty soon now.

OLLIE: Don't pay him no mind.

JIM: Naw. There's a wall between him an' me.

BUTCH: You bet there is. Or you'd be a dead Canary. There'd be yellow feathers floating all over Hall C!

JIM [*exhaling smoke as he speaks—à la Jules Garfield**]: There's a wall like that around ev'ry man in here an' outside of here, Ollie.

OLLIE: Outside? Naw!

JIM: Sure there is. Ev'ry man living is walking around in a cage. He carries it with him wherever he goes and don't let it go till he's dead. Then the walls come to pieces and he stops being lonesome—

[*Butch grins delightedly and nudges Joe; he describes a circle with his finger and points at Jim's cell. They both crouch grinning, listening, on the bench by the wall.*]

—Cause he's part of something bigger than him.

OLLIE: Bigger than him?

JIM: Yes.

---

*John Garfield, actor, whose real name was Julius Garfinkle, was known as Jules Garfield on the stage. The 1938 film *Four Daughters* features him smoking, a cigarette dangling from his mouth.

OLLIE: What's that?

JIM [*blowing an enormous smoke ring and piercing it with his finger*]: The Universe!

[*Butch erupts in hoarse derisive laughter.*]

JIM [*ignoring Butch's outburst*]: But, sometimes, I think, Ollie, a guy don't have to wait till he's dead to get outside of his cage.

OLLIE: Yuh mean he should bump himself off?

JIM: No. A guy can use his brain two ways. He can make it a wall to shut him in from the world or a great big door to let him out. [*He continues musingly.*] Intellectual emancipation!

OLLIE: Huh?

[*Butch gives a long whistle.*]

OLLIE: What's that?

JIM: Couple of words I came across in a book.

OLLIE: Sound like big words.

JIM: They *are* big words. So big that the *world* hangs on 'em. They can tell us what to read, what to say, what to do— But they can't tell us what to *think*! And as long as man can think as he pleases he's never exactly locked up anywhere. He can think himself outside of all their walls and boundaries and make the world his place to live in— It's a swell feeling, Ollie, when you've done that. It's like being alone on the top of a mountain at night with nothing around you but stars. Only you're not alone, though, cause you know that you're part of everything living and everything living is part of you. Then you get an idea of what God is. Not Mr. Santie Claus, Ollie, dropping answers to prayers down chimneys—

OLLIE: Naw?

JIM: No, not that. But something big and terrible as night is, and yet—

OLLIE: Huh?

JIM: And yet—as soft as a woman. Y'see what I mean?

BUTCH: I see whatcha mean—it's kind of a—*balmy* feeling! [*Butch and Joe laugh. Jim looks resentfully at wall.*]

JIM: You guys don't get what I'm talking about.

OLLIE [*musingly*]: Naw, but I do. Thinkin's like prayin', excep' that prayin' yuh feel like yuh've got some one on the other end a th' line. . .

JIM [*smiling*]: Yeah.

[*The spot fades on Jim's cell and focuses on Butch's.*]

QUEEN: Be quiet, you *all*. I'm sick. I need my sleep. [*He mutters to himself.*]

[*A searchlight from river shines on the window.*]

JOE: Where's that light from?

BUTCH [*at the window*]: Anudder boat load a goddam jitter-bugs. Dey're trowin th' glims on us. Whaddaya think this is? Th' Municipal Zoo or something? Go to hell, yuh sons-a-bitches, yuh lousy—

SCHULTZ [*rapping at the bars with a stick*]: After lights in there!

BUTCH: Someday it's gonna be permanuntly 'after lights' for that old screw.

JOE [*twisting on bed*]: Oooooo!

BUTCH: Bellyache?

JOE: Yeah, from them stinkin' meatballs. By God I'm gonna quit eatin' if they don't start puttin' in more digestable food.

BUTCH [*reflectively*]: Quit eating, huh? —I think yuh got something there.

JOE: Oooooo—*Christ*! [*He draws his knees up to his chin.*}

BUTCH: You ever heard of a hunger-strike, Joe?

JOE: Uh.

BUTCH: Sometimes it works. Gits in the papers. Starts inves-tigations. They git better food.

JOE: Oooooo! We'd git—*uh*!—*Klondike*!

BUTCH: Klondike won't hold thirty-five hundred men.

JOE: No. But Hall C would go first on account of our reputation.

BUTCH: Okay. We'll beat Klondike.

JOE: You talk too big sometimes. You ever been in Klondike?

BUTCH: Yeah. Once.

JOE: What's it like?

BUTCH: It's a little suburb of hell.

JOE: That's what I thought.

BUTCH: They got radiators all aroun' the walls an' there ain't no windows.

JOE: Christ Almighty!

BUTCH: Steam hisses outa the valves like this. [*He imitates the sound.*] Till it gits so thick you can't see nothing around you. It's like breathin' fire in yer lungs. The floor is so hot you can't stand on it, but there's no place else to stand—

JOE: How do yuh live?

BUTCH: There's an air hole about this size at the bottom of the wall. But when there's a bunch in Klondike they git panicky an' fight over the air hole an' the ones that ain't strong don't make it.

JOE: It kills 'em?

41

BUTCH: Sure. Unless the Boss takes 'em out. And when you beat Klondike you beat everything they've got to offer in here. It's their Ace of Spades!

QUEEN [*rising sleepily on his bunk*]: What's that about Klondike, Butch?

JOE: Nothing. He's talking in his sleep.

QUEEN: I dreamed about Klondike one night.

JOE: Did ja?

QUEEN: Sure. That was the night I woke up screaming. Remember?

JOE: Sure. I remember. —Oooooo! Uhhhhhh! Ahhhhhh! Jesus! [*He springs out of bed and crouches on the floor, clasping his stomach.*]

BLACKOUT

Announcer: "Band Music!"

Theme up: Tchaikovsky, "1812 Overture," 2nd Theme. Fade.

A spot comes up on the office. Jim is settled comfortably in a chair by the window, writing. Eva enters.

EVA [*brightly*]: Good morning.

JIM: Hi.

EVA [*removing her hat, etc.*]: I believe you spend more time here than the boss does.

JIM: I like it here. Especially when I'm alone.

EVA: Oh—well, excuse my intrusion.

JIM: I don't mean you. You don't bother me [*His immediate tension at her entrance belies this.*]

EVA: Thanks.

JIM [*watching her as she removes the cover from the machine*]: As a matter of fact it's a rare and enviable privilege for a connie to get close to a member of the opposite sex.

EVA: Really?

JIM: Yes. Really and truly. I have to blink my eyes a couple of times to be sure you're not just one of them—visual and auditory hallucinations—that some fellows develop in stir.

EVA [*inserting a form-sheet in the typewriter*]: Wasn't there a girl working here before me?

JIM: There was. But she wasn't nearly such a strain upon one's—credulity.

EVA: How do you mean?

JIM: She was sort of a cow.

EVA: Oh.

JIM: Whalen's wife's second cousin. But he's a remarkable man.

EVA [*whose typing obscured the last phrase*]: He is or she is?

JIM: They both were. [*He laughs.*] Now you know why I'm called the Canary. I talk too much.

EVA: No. In what way?

JIM [*thumbing toward the inner room*]: He had her in there the first week.

EVA: What's in there?

JIM: He goes in there to relax after ground-inspection. She would go in there with him. —She died of an operation and Whalen bought his wife a mink coat. How do you like your new job?

EVA: Well! —Not so good now.

JIM: There's some features of life on the grounds that aren't mentioned in the *Sunday Supplement*.

EVA: Yes. I didn't sleep last night.

JIM: No?

EVA: From thinking about that boy's mother.

JIM: You'll get used to things like that.

EVA: I don't want to get used to them.

JIM: Why don't you quit, then?

EVA: Say! You don't know much about the unemployment situation.

JIM: No. I got here before the Depression.

EVA: You're lucky.

JIM: Think so?

EVA: There was a case in the paper where a man busted a plate-glass window so he could go to jail and get something to eat.

JIM: I bet he regretted it afterwards. Especially if he came here.

EVA: I don't know. The sample menu's okay.

JIM: Huh! We spill that stuff on everybody comes in the office to cover up what's actually going on.

EVA [*removing the form-sheet*]: What's that?

JIM: Starvation.

EVA: You're crazy!

JIM: Sure I am, crazy as a bedbug! But I've still got sense enough to recognize beans an' hamburger an' spaghetti—when I see them six or seven times a week in slightly variegated combinations! You wonder why we make such a fuss about eating? Well, I'll tell you why. It's because eating's all we got. We got nothing else, no women to sleep with, no hammers, no shovels, no papers to write on, no automobiles, no golf—nothin' to do but eat—so eating's important to us. And when they make that so darned monotonous that you feel like puking at the sight of it—then they're putting the match to a keg of powder! [*He lights his cigarette.*] Ask me what is a pyrotechnical display!

EVA: I think I know.

JIM: You'll know better if you stick around. We're going to have the loveliest Fourth o'July you ever laid eyes on. Only it's going to come, maybe in the middle of August. Y'see I've got my ear to the ground—in here and in Hall C— This place, lady, is the practical equivalent of Mt. Vesuvius. Maybe a hundred years from now little woolly white lambs will be grazing peacefully on the slopes of an extinct volcano. But down at the bottom tourist guides will be pointing out the bones of people who didn't get out of Pompeii!

EVA: Too bad you won't be one of the guides. You make such good speeches.

JIM: Okay. Be funny about it.

[*The sound of a brass band playing a martial air in the assembly hall is heard.*]*

EVA [*her face brightening*]: Band music!

JIM: Yes. They're practicing for the Commissioner's banquet.

EVA [*rising*]: Sounds very gay!

JIM: Uh-huh. If you believed in brass bands you'd think the millennium was going to arrive at exactly 6 A.M. tomorrow.

EVA [*facing him with desperate gaiety*]: Why not? Maybe it will! —A brass band can sell me *anything*, Jim!

JIM: Can it sell you this? [*He catches her against him in a hard impulsive embrace.*]

EVA [*breaking away*]: Yes, it could even sell me that! [*Then she laughs.*] —But not in the Warden's office! [*She goes quickly back to her typing— Jim stands motionless looking at her back—his arms raised slowly—the hands clench into fists— they vibrate, outstretched, with a terrific intensity—then slowly fall to his sides. Eva whistles gaily to the band music.*]

DIM OUT

---

*In the margin of his original typescript Williams has written: "Bells in the Burning City— 1812 Overture—Tschaikovsky." This seems to relate to Jim's mention of fireworks and the 4th of July, Independence Day, when the *Festival Overture* is traditionally performed in the United States. The symphony's ending with the sound of canon fire is the signal for a fireworks display.

Announcer: "Mister Olympics!"

A spot comes up on the cell. Men have just returned from supper.

JOE: Did you eat yours?

BUTCH: Eat that stuff? Naw. It made me sick to look at it.

JOE: Spaghetti four times a week!

BUTCH: That's nutten. I useta work in a spaghetti factory.

QUEEN: Really?

BUTCH: Yeah. I remember one time the spaghetti machines got out of control. We couldn't stop 'em. The whole place was full of spaghetti. It was spaghetti ev'rywhere, oozin' out of the floor an' the walls, an' the ceilin', spaghetti, spaghetti, blockin' up the windows an' the doors, a big suffocatin' mass of spaghetti.

QUEEN: Please!

BUTCH: So I says to the foreman, "For Chrissakes, how we gonna git outa this place wit' all this spaghetti sloppin' aroun' ev'rywhere?" —An' the boss says, "Boys—there's only one way to git out of here now!" —"How's that?" I ast him. —"Here!" he says—an' he han's me a big knife an' fork—"Yuh got to *EAT* yuh way out!"

QUEEN: Oh, for the love of nasturtiums!

[*The steel doors clang.*]

VOICE: Hello, new boy! [*Other greetings are given.*]

BUTCH: They're bringin' a new boy in.

[*Schultz stops in front of the cell with Swifty.*]

SCHULTZ: Here's yer boudoir, Sonny.

SWIFTY: Here?

SCHULTZ: Yeah. Here. [*He shoves him roughly in and slams the door.*]

SWIFTY: What did he do that for? Shove me! I was going in, wasn't I?

JOE: Sure you was going in. He just wanted to help you.

SWIFTY: I don't like being pushed around like that.

JOE: I'd complain to the Governor.

SWIFTY [*pausing as he looks about*]: I've got an appeal coming before the Governor.

JOE: Have you now?

SWIFTY: Yes, I didn't get a fair trial. I was railroaded up here. My lawyer said so.

JOE: Your lawyer said so.

SWIFTY: Yes, he said— Hey, do we all stay in here together like this? Jeez, it's too small!

49

JOE: What's that your lawyer said?

SWIFTY: He said— What's that? A cockroach! Gosh—I don't like being cooped up like this!

JOE: What did your lawyer say?

SWIFTY: He said for me to sit tight. He'd have me out of here in two weeks, a month at the most.

JOE: A month at the most! What do you think of that, Butch?

BUTCH: I think it's a lot of what they use shovels to clean off the stable floor! [*He rises.*] —That's your new bunk, new boy. Get up there an' lissen to what I tell yuh. —Go on!

SWIFTY: Quit shoving!

BUTCH: Huh?

SWIFTY: I told you I don't like being pushed around!

BUTCH [*exhibiting his fists*]: When you talk back to me you're talking back to this! —Now git up there an' pay attention to what I say.

SWIFTY: Why should I take orders from you? You're not one of the officials around here.

BUTCH: Ain't I?

SWIFTY: No!

BUTCH: Lissen, buddy. In Spain, it's Mussolini.

JOE: You mean Italy it's Mussolini.

BUTCH: I mean wherever there's wops! An' in Germany it's that monkey wit' the trick mustache! —But in here it's Butch O'Fallon! And Butch O'Fallon is me! So now that we've been properly introduced I would like to repeat my polite invitation to remove your butt from my bunk an' git up in your own! [*Butch jerks Swifty up by the collar and hoists him by the seat of his pants to the upper bunk.*] What's yuh name?

SWIFTY: Jeremy Trout.

BUTCH: This yuh first stretch?

SWIFTY: Yes. What of it?

BUTCH: What's yuh rap?

SWIFTY: I was indicted for—stealing—money.

BUTCH: What from?

SWIFTY: Cash register in a chain store. I was cashier. But I didn't do it. I was framed by a couple of clerks.

BUTCH: I believe you. You don't look like you'd have gumption enough to crack a till. How much you got?

SWIFTY: On me? Nothing. They even took my cigarettes.

BUTCH: I mean your stretch. How long?

SWIFTY: Judge Eggleston gave me five years. But my lawyer says—

BUTCH: You'll *do* five years.

SWIFTY: In here? Why, I'd go crazy locked in here that long!

BUTCH: Pocket yuh marbles!

SWIFTY: I—I feel sick. The air in here's no good.

BUTCH: No?

SWIFTY: It smells. It's making me sick at the stomach.

BUTCH: There's the slop bucket.

SWIFTY: No!

BUTCH: It ain't been emptied yet. That's your job. The new man always empties.

SWIFTY: No— [*He sinks into his bunk.*] —Five years? I couldn't stand being cooped up that long. I got to have space around me. I get restless. That's why I didn't like working in the chain store. Kept me behind a counter all day, felt like I was tied up there. —At high school I was a runner.

BUTCH: A runner, huh?

QUEEN: That's what I said to myself. He looks athletic.

SWIFTY: Yes. I held the 220 state record for three years.

BUTCH: Fancy that.

SWIFTY: I like anything that's moving, that don't stay put. It's not an ordinary thing with me, it's kind of an obsession. I like to kill distance. See a straight track—get to the other end of it first, before anyone else— That's what I was made for—running—look at my legs!

JOE: Pips, huh?

SWIFTY: That's from training. If this hadn't happened I'd be on my way to the Olympics right now. I could still have a chance at the New York eliminations if my lawyer can spring me before the fifteenth. [*He flexes his legs.*] —But look at that! Getting loose already! —If I could get permission to run around the yard a few times—say, before breakfast or supper—why, I could keep in pretty good shape even in here. Even if I had to stay in here a year—that way I could keep in condition!

JOE: He'll go like Sailor Jack.

BUTCH: Pocket yuh marbles! —Buddy, I ain't sentimental— but I feel sorry for you.

SWIFTY: Why? Don't you think he'll let me?

BUTCH: Naw.

SWIFTY: Why not?

BUTCH: Because you're a con.

SWIFTY: But a con's a human being. He's got to be treated like one.

BUTCH: A con ain't a human being. A con's a con. [*The lights fade on the others and concentrate on Butch.*] He's stuck in here and the world's forgot him. As far as the world is concerned he don't exist anymore. What happens to him in here—them people outside don't know, they don't care. He's entrusted to the care of the State. The State? Hell! The State turns him over to a guy called a Warden and a bunch of other guys called guards. Who're they? Men who like to boss other men. Maybe they could've been truckdrivers or street cleaners or circus clowns. But they didn't wanta be none a them. Why? Cause they've got a natural instinck for swinging a shelailee! They like to crack heads, make sausage out of human flesh! And so they get to be guards. That sounds like 'gods'—which ain't so much a coincidence either, because the only diff'rence between 'guards' an' 'gods' is that 'guards' has an 'r' in it an' the 'r' stands for 'rat'! —That's what a guard is accordin' to my definition— 'A rat who thinks that he's GOD!' —You better not forget that. Because, Sonny, you're not in high school no more. You ain't in the chain store, you're not at the Olympics— That's Part One of your education. Part Two is stay away from stool pigeons. Hey, Canary! —He ain't in yet but we got a little songbird in the next cage who sings real sweetly sometimes for the boss. —So don't be buddies wit him. Give 'im a cigarette, Joe.

JOE: Here, mister Olympics.

BUTCH: Keep it covered. —How's yuh stomach now?

SWIFTY: Some better.

BUTCH: Hungry?

SWIFTY: No.

BUTCH: That's good. Because we might quit eating.

QUEEN: Quit eating?

BUTCH: Yep. I been thinkin' over what we talked about las' night, Joe, an' I'm just about sold on it.

JOE: I'm still on the fence about that.

BUTCH: There ain't any fence to be on, Joe. When I say hunger strike in here it's going to be hunger strike.

QUEEN: Hunger strike!

SWIFTY: What's that?

BUTCH: Pocket yuh marbles. The Canary's comin' to roost.

[*Derisive whistles are heard in the hall.*]

Help me off wit' these shoes, Queenie. That's right. Here, hang up my shirt. Joe—

JOE: What the hell?

BUTCH: You fold my pants up nice an' lay 'em over the chair. —Hello, moon. [*He stands in a shaft of moonlight through the barred window.*]

JOE: You're going like Sailor Jack, saying hello to the moon!

BUTCH: She's big an' yellow tonight. Y'know me an' God have got something in common, Joe.

JOE: Yeah, what's that?

BUTCH: A weakness for blondes!

BLACKOUT

Announcer: "Butch Has A Dream."

Theme up: "Roses of Picardy." Fade.

GOLDIE: Hello, Butch.

BUTCH [*half-rising on his bunk*]: Goldie!

GOLDIE: Yes, it's me.

BUTCH: How didja get in here?

GOLDIE: Walls ain't thick enough to keep us apart always, Butch.

BUTCH: You mean you walked right through? They couldn't stop you?

GOLDIE: That's right, honey.

BUTCH: It's marvelous, marvelous!

GOLDIE: Sure. I never was an ordinary bim. There was always something unusual about me. You noticed that. How light I was on my feet and always laughing. A girl that danced like me, all night till they wrapped up the fiddles and covered the drums, that never got tired, that always wanted one more of whatever was offered, is something kind of special. You know that, Butch. You don't buy us two for a quarter at the corner drug.

BUTCH: Yeah, I know that, Goldie. I always had that special feeling about you, kid. Honey, I used to try to find words to tell yuh what you did to me nights when you opened your mouth against mine and give me your love. . .

Room twenty-three! That was yours. Six flights up the narrow stairs with brass tacks in an old red carpet and bulbs at the end of the hall. Fire-escape. We used to sit out there summer nights and drink iced beer till all we could do was giggle and then go to bed.

Day used to come so slow and easy through the long white blinds. Maybe a little wind making the curtains stir. The milk wagons rattled along, and out on the East River the fog horns blew. I never slept, I lay and watched you sleeping. Your face was like the face of a little girl then. A girl no man ever touched. I never told you about those time I watched you sleeping and how I felt toward you then. Because I wasn't good at making speeches. But I guess you knew.

GOLDIE: Of course I knew. I knew you loved me, Butch.

BUTCH: I wonder if your face still looks like that when you're sleeping.

GOLDIE: I haven't changed. You oughta know that, Butch.

BUTCH: You don't go out with other fellows, do you?

GOLDIE: No. You know I don't. I been as true as God to you, Butch.

BUTCH: But how do you live, how do you get along now, Goldie?

GOLDIE: As good as a girl can expect. I still work days over at the Imperial Dry Cleaners and nights I work at the Paradise, Butch.

BUTCH: I wanted you to quit the Paradise, Goldie.

GOLDIE: What for?

BUTCH: I don't like other guys dancin' witcha.

GOLDIE: They don't mean nothing. Just pasteboard tickets, that's all they are to me, Butch. I keep the stubs an' turn 'em in for cash. And that's as far as it goes.

BUTCH: But when they hold you close sometimes when the lights go out for the waltz—you don't ever close your eyes and blow your breath on their necks like you done for me, Goldie?

GOLDIE: No. Never.

BUTCH: You wouldn't lie to me, Goldie?

GOLDIE: Of course I wouldn't. Some of the girls say one man's as good as another. They're all the same. But I'm not made like that. I give myself, I give myself for *keeps*. And time don't change me none. I'm still the same.

BUTCH: The same old Goldie, huh?

GOLDIE: The same old kid. Running my dancing slippers down at the heels. But not forgetting your love. And going home nights alone. Sleeping alone in a big brass bed. Half of it empty, Butch. And waiting for you.

BUTCH: Waiting for me!

GOLDIE: Yes! Waiting for you! [*She begins to fade into the shadows.*]

BUTCH [*reaching toward her*]: Goldie!

GOLDIE: So long, Butch. So long. . .

BUTCH [*frantically*]: Goldie! Goldie! [*She has completely disappeared.*]

JOE [*sitting up on his bunk*]: What's the matter, Butch.

QUEEN: He's talkin' in his sleep again.

BUTCH [*slowly and with terrific emphasis*]: God—damn!

BLACKOUT

Announcer: "A Rubber Duck for the Baby!"

A spot comes up on the Warden's office. The Boss is seated at his desk inflating a rubber duck.

WARDEN [*to Eva who lays papers on his desk*]: Look at this.

EVA: Yes.

WARDEN: It's a rubber duck for the baby.

EVA: I didn't know you had one.

WARDEN: You bet I got one. Cutest little baby doll you ever set eyes on!

EVA: Boy or girl?

WARDEN: Girl! Wouldn't have nothing else. Will she be tickled when she sees this! [*Eva starts to leave.*] Wait! I'm gonna git her on the phone now! You wanta hear this, Eva? [*He dials.*] Hello, Mama? How's tricks? Yeah? Well, put the baby on, will yuh? [*To Eva*]: Now lissen to this! Puddikins? Popsy dust wanted to know if oo was bein' a dood little durl! Oo are? Dat's dood. Popsy'd dot somefin fo dood little durls! No. Not a stick-candies. Oo see when Popsy dets home, 'es oo will! Bye-bye now! Bye-bye!— [*He hangs up with a chuckle.*] Cute 's the dickens—looks just like Shirley Temple—don't she though? [*He shows a picture to Eva.*]

EVA: Yes, there is a resemblance.

[*Jim enters.*]

WARDEN [*heartily*]: Hello, Jimmy boy! What's new?

JIM: Nothing new. Just the same old complaints about food. Only they're getting louder all the time, Boss.

WARDEN: What do they want? Caviar? Cream puffs? Charlotte Russes? Do they want us to have printed menus so they can order their meals *à la carte*? Stick these medical reports in the file case, Eva.

JIM: If you look those reports over you'll see there was seven cases of ptomaine poisoning after the Wednesday night supper. Those meatballs were worse on the stomach than they were on the nose!

WARDEN: What do you mean? They weren't good?

JIM: I think they were meant for the buzzards out at the zoo. Got mixed up at the market or something and came over here by mistake.

WARDEN: Look here, Jim. You're talking too uppity. Showing off for Miss Crane, I guess—'s at it?

JIM: No, Sir. If I didn't give you my honest opinion what good would I be?

WARDEN [*slowly, studying Jim's face*]: Okay. Yeah, you're a good boy, Jim.

JIM: Thanks.

WARDEN [*leaning back*]: I like you, Jim. Why? Cause you got a face that looks like it was cut outa rock. Turn sideways, Jim— Eva?

EVA [at the files]: Yes, Sir?

WARDEN: Ever seen a cleaner-cut profile than that? Like it was carved in stone, huh? Them jaws, the nose, the mouth? I tried to break that when Jim first come in here. Never did. It stayed like it is—stone face! Never got it to change, not even when I give him fifty stripes with a rubber hose ev'ry morning for fourteen days. —Remember that, Jim?

JIM [his face barely tightening]: Yes, Sir.

WARDEN: When I seen I couldn't break him I said to myself, "Hey, Bert, here's a man you could use!" So I did. Jim's a trusty, now, a stool pigeon—Canary Jim—that's what the other cons all call him. Ain't that so, Jim?

JIM: Yes, Sir.

WARDEN: Keeps me posted on conditions among the men. He don't come gum-shoeing, whispering like the other stool pigeons I got in here—he comes straight out and says what he thinks! —That's what makes him valuable to me! —But the men don't like him. They hate your guts, don't they, Jim?

JIM: Yes, Sir. [He speaks in almost a whisper.]

WARDEN: Jim's on my side, all right. I couldn't break him so I made him useful. Take off your shirt, Jim—show Eva your back.

JIM: Yes, Sir. [He obeys with curious, machine-like precision. Diagonally across his shoulder down to the waist are long scars which ten years could not obliterate.]

WARDEN: See them scars, Eva? He got them ten years ago. Pretty sight he was then. Raw meat. The skin hung down from his back like pieces of red tissue paper! The flesh was all pulpy, beat up, the blood squirted out like juice from a ripe tomato ev'ry time I brung the whip down on him. "Had enough, Jim? Ready to go back to that embossing machine?" —"Naw," says Jim, —"Not till it's fixed!" —He defied me like that for four-teen days.—I seen I'd either have to kill him or I'd have to admit that he had me licked.—I says to him, "Jim, you win! You don't go back to that embossing machine, you stay right here in the office an' work for me because you're a man that's made out of stuff that I like!" Stone face! Huh, Jim?

JIM: Yes, Sir. [*The papers have already slipped from Eva's hands. She utters a slight breathless cry and grips the edge of the desk.*]

WARDEN: Thunderation! What's wrong?

JIM: I think she's fainting. [*He catches Eva.*]

WARDEN: Let go of that girl—get your shirt on and get out. —Tell the boys in Hall C I'm tired a complaints about food. —Well, young lady?

EVA: I'm all right now.

WARDEN: Awright, I've got her. —Get your shirt back on, Jim—I want you to have a little talk with Butch O'Fallon tonight. —Tell him I'm tired a complaints in Hall C, and if he wants trouble I'm the baby that can dish it out! —Go on, get on out!

JIM: Yes, Sir. [*He exits slowly.*]

63

WARDEN [*to Eva who has sunk in her chair*]. Well, young lady?

EVA: I'm all right now.

WARDEN: Sorry. I didn't mean to make it that strong. Jim's a good boy, but it don't hurt to remind him once in a while of his old friend Dr. Jones.

[*Eva averts her face.*]

You think I'm brutal, dontcha? You got to realize the position I'm in. I got thirty-five hundred men here, men that would knife their own mothers for the price of a beer. It takes a mighty firm hand.—Yes, Siree! [*He picks up the rubber duck—inflates it some more.*] Cute, huh? —She'll make a fuss over this!

DIM OUT

Announcer: "Explosion!"

The spot comes up on the cell. We should feel a definite increase of tension over the preceding cell scenes. Butch paces restlessly. The others sit sullenly on their bunks, the Queen with an old movie magazine, Swifty anxiously flexing his legs.

JOE [*entering from the hall and removing the jacket*]: Save your shoe leather.

BUTCH: What for?

JOE: You might want to eat it tonight instead of cold beans.

BUTCH: Beans, huh?

SWIFTY [*with a letter*]: It's from my lawyer.

QUEEN: What's he say, honey?

SWIFTY: He says for me to sit tight.

QUEEN: Goodness! —My nails are in awful condition.

SWIFTY: Sit tight! What does he think I've been doing since I got here? Sit tight—sit tight! Don't he know I've got to be moving around?

BUTCH: Take it easy, Mister Olympics! —Who toleja cold beans?

JOE: Boy that works in the kitchen.

SWIFTY: I don't trust that lawyer. This time he says six months.

QUEEN: I don't trust no man, honey. No further'n I could kick Grant's Tomb with a fractured toe! [*He giggles.*]

BUTCH: He oughta know.

SWIFTY: My lawyer?

BUTCH: Your lawyer! Naw—the kitchen boy.

JOE: Maybe our friend the Canary forgot to spill.

BUTCH: He'd never forget to spill anything.

JOE: Then maybe the Boss don't care how we feel about cold beans for supper.

BUTCH: He wants to call our hand.

JOE: Sure. He's got an ace in the hole. —Klondike!

BUTCH: We've got one, too.

JOE: Hunger strike?

BUTCH: You named it, Brother.

JOE: Two guys can't hold the ace of spades.

BUTCH: Once I sat in a game where that was the situation.

JOE: How didja solve it?

BUTCH [*producing his razor*]: Wit' this.

JOE: You better quit flashin' that thing.

BUTCH: Ev'rybody knows I got tough whiskers. [*He laughs and replaces razor in his belt.*] "Fawchun's always hid-ing—/ I looked ev'rywhere!"

[*Bird calls are heard from the hall.*]

Here it comes, it's th' Canary. [*He gives a shrill whistle.*] Hello, Canary. How's them solo flights you been makin? You know—out there on the mountain tops wit' nothing around ja but the stars? [*He and Joe laugh.*]

OLLIE [*from next cell*]: Don't pay 'em no mind, Jim.

JIM: Never mind about that. I got something to tell you.

BUTCH: Tell us about Goldilocks and the bears.

JOE: I like Goody-Two-Shoes.

JIM: Come outside for a minute.

BUTCH: You wanta fight?

JIM: No, I wanta talk.

BUTCH: You allus wanta talk, that's your trouble. If you got something to spill come in here.

JIM: I know what happened last time I got in a cage with you, Butch.

BUTCH: I'm glad I made that good an impression.

JIM: Are you coming out?

BUTCH: Naw. Are you coming in?

JIM: Yeah. I will. Soon as they douse the glims.

QUEEN: Better not, honey. Butch has got tough whiskers.

JIM: Yeah, I know what he cuts 'em with.

BUTCH: Why dontcha spill it, then?

JIM: I never deliberately ratted on nobody, Butch.

[*A whistle sounds. The lights dim.*]

Okay. I'm coming in now. [*He unlocks the cell and enters.*]

QUEEN: Now, Butch—

JOE: Watch, yourself. It's not worth getting jerked to Jesus for.

BUTCH: Naw, Canary, my respect for you is increased two hundred percent. I never thought you'd have what it takes to step inside here.

JIM: It's like what I was telling Ollie last night. We've all got walls around ourselves, Butch, that we can't see through—that's why we make so many mistakes about each other. Have a smoke?

BUTCH: Naw. Just say what you got to say and then take a double powder. I don't wanta lose control.

JIM: I know what you've got in mind.

BUTCH: What?

JIM: Hunger strike.

BUTCH: What of it?

JIM: I don't recommend it, Butch.

BUTCH: Did Whalen tell you to say that?

JIM: Naw, this is on the level, Butch.

BUTCH: Yeah, about as level as the Adirondacks.

JIM: I'll admit I've made myself useful to him. But I haven't forgotten two weeks we spent in the Hole together, and those visits he paid every morning to inquire about our health. He was even more solicitous about mine than yours, Butch. Things like that can make a common bond between men that nothing afterwards can ever—

BUTCH: Come to the point!

JIM: All right. I'm coming up for parole next month.

BUTCH [*rising*]: You are, huh?

JIM: There's a chance I might get it. And if I do I'm going to justify my reputation as a brilliant vocalist, Butch. I'm going to sing so loud and so high that the echo will knock these walls down! I know plenty from working in the office. I know all the pet grafts. I know all about the intimidation of employees and torture of convicts; I know about the Hole, about the water cure, about the overcoat—about Klondike! —And I know about the kind of food—or slop, rather!—that we been eating! You wait a month! That's all! When I get through Whalen will be where he belongs—in the psychopathic ward with Sailor Jack! And I promise you things will change in here—look—here's an article about the Industrial Reformatory in Chillicothe!—that's the kind of a place this'll be!

BUTCH [*throwing the paper aside*]: I don't want no articles! —Allison, you're full of shit.

JOE: Take it easy, Butch. [*To Jim.*] So you don't want us to go on hunger strike?

JIM: No. It won't do any good. The Boss'll throw the bunch of you in Klondike. Do yourself a favor. Work with me. We can case this jug. But not if we keep on going opposite ways. —Give me your hand on it, Butch.

BUTCH: Fuck you!

JIM: It's no dice, huh? What do you say, Joe? Swifty?

BUTCH: They say what I say! Now git out before I lose my last ounce a restriction!

JIM: Okay. [*He goes out.*]

JOE: Maybe he *was* on the level.

BUTCH: He will be on the level when he's laid out straight under ground. [*He slaps Swifty's rump.*] Git up! It's supper time!

SWIFTY [*his face buried in the pillow*]: Leave me alone. I'm sick. I'm not hungry.

BUTCH: You're coming along anyhow. We need you to help make some noise in case the kitchen boy was right about supper.

JOE: Noise?

BUTCH: Yep, *plenty* of noise!

[*The bell rings in the hall.*]

BUTCH: Come along, youse! [*He shoves Queen and jerks Swifty to his feet.*] Hell's bells are ringin'! Come on, boys! Before them biscuits git cold! T-bone steaks for supper! Smothered in mushrooms! Come and git it!

[*A whistle is heard and the lights dim out. Theme up: "1812 Overture." Fade.*]

BLACKOUT

Announcer: "Hell—an Expressionistic Interlude"

The following scene takes place on a dark stage. The shuffling of feet is heard and continues for several moments. A whistle sounds.

VOICE: TAKE PLACES AT TABLES! [*More shuffling is heard.*] Set down!

[*Now we hear the scrape of chairs or benches as the men sit.*]

VOICE: Start eating!

[*A low yammering commences.*]

VOICE: Start eating, I said! You heard me! Start eating!

[*Very softly, in a whisper, voices begin to be heard, transmitting a message from table to table with rising intensity.*]

VOICES: Quit eating—quit eating—quit eating—quit eating—don't eat no more a dis slop—trow it back in deir faces—quit eating—quit eating—we don't eat crap—we're human—quit eating—QUIT EATING—

[*The chorus grows louder, more hysterical, becomes like the roaring of animals. As the yammering swells there is a clatter of tin cups. The lights come up on Butch and others seated on benches at a table. Each has a tin cup and plate with which he beats time to the chorus of the Chant led by Ollie, who stands, stage forward, in the spotlight.*]

OLLIE: Devil come to meet us an' he rang on a bell,
Twenty-five men got a ticket to hell!

CHORUS: Turn on the heat, turn on the heat,
　　　　They're gonna give us hell when they turn on the
　　　　　heat.
　　　　Turn on the heat, turn on the heat,
　　　　They're gonna give us hell when they turn on the
　　　　　heat.

OLLIE: Down in Mizzoura where I was born
　　　　I worked all day in a field of corn,
　　　　Got pretty hot but at night it was nice
　　　　'Cause we kept our beer in a bucket of ice.

CHORUS: Turn on the heat, turn on the heat,
　　　　They're gonna give us hell when they turn on the
　　　　　heat.
　　　　Turn on the heat, turn on the heat,
　　　　They're gonna give us hell when they turn on the
　　　　　heat.

BUTCH: There's one rap that a connie can't beat
　　　　When the Warden says, Boys, we gonna turn on the
　　　　　heat!

CHORUS: Turn on the heat, turn on the heat,
　　　　They're gonna give us hell when they turn on the
　　　　　heat.

OLLIE: Devil come to meet us an' he rang on a bell,
　　　　Twenty-five men got a ticket to HELL!

CHORUS: Turn on the heat, turn on the heat,
　　　　They're gonna give us hell when they turn on the
　　　　　heat.

Turn on the heat, turn on the heat,
They're gonna give us hell when they turn on the
heat.

[*The lights fade. There is a loud ringing of bells: a whistle sounds; then a sudden dead silence. The lights fade and come up on Schultz and the guards, entering cellblock. The prisoners are back in their cells.*]

SCHULTZ: Now you boys are gonna learn a good lesson about makin' disturbances in mess hall! Git one out of each cell! Keep 'em covered!

JOE [*to Butch*]: You started something all right.

QUEEN: Oh, Lord!

SCHULTZ: Ollie! Shapiro! Come on out, you're elected! Mex!

SHAPIRO: What for! Distoibance? I make no distoibance!

MEX: [*He protests volubly in Spanish.*]

OLLIE: What you want me fo', Mistuh Schultz?

SCHULTZ [*at the door of Butch's cell*]: Stand back there, Butch. [*He prods him with a gun.*] Who's in here with you? Joe? Queenie?

BUTCH: I started the noise.

SCHULTZ: I know you started the noise. But we're saving you, Butch. You're too good to waste on the Hole.

QUEEN: I didn't make any noise, Mr. Schultz. I was perfectly quiet the whole time.

SCHULTZ: Who's that on the bunk? Aw, the new boy. Playing Puss-in-the-Corner! Come on out.

QUEEN: He didn't make noise, Mr. Schultz.

SCHULTZ: Come out, boy!

SWIFTY [shaking]: I didn't make any noise. I was sick. I didn't want any supper. I've been sick ever since I come here.

SCHULTZ: Yes, I've heard you squawking! Git in line there.

SWIFTY: I wanta see the Warden. It makes me sick being shut up without exercise.

SCHULTZ: We'll exercise you! [He blows a whistle.]

SWIFTY [wildly]: The Hole? No! No!

SCHULTZ [prodding him roughly with a billy]: Git moving! Krause! Alberts! Awright, that's all! —Two weeks in the hole, bread an' water—maybe we'll finish off with a Turkish bath. —Step on it, Mex!

MEX: [He swears in Spanish.]

SHAPIRO: Distoibance? Not me. Naw.

SCHULTZ: Hep, hep, hep— [A slow shuffling is heard as the lights begin to dim.]

JOE: Christ!

QUEEN: Swifty won't make it! They'll kill him down there!

[*The whistle is heard, then the distant clang of steel.*]

BUTCH [*whistles a few bars then sings out*]:
    They fly so high, nearly reach the sky
    Then like my dreams they fade an' die!
    Fawchun's always hiding—I looked ev'rywhere!

[*Theme up and dim out.*]

MEX: [*He protests in Spanish.*]

SCHULTZ: Fall in line! March! Hep, hep, hep— [*The voice diminishes as they move, heads bent, shoulders sagging, shuffling down the corridor.*]

BLACKOUT SLOWLY

Announcer: "Hunger Strike!"

A spot comes up on the office. Eva enters.

WARDEN: Had your supper?

EVA: Yes.

WARDEN [*watching her as she crosses downstage*]: Hate to keep you overtime like this—but with the boys in Hall C kicking up such a rumpus, we got to have all our books in perfect shape—just in case the professional snoopers git on our tails about something!

EVA: Yes Sir. [*She removes the cover from the typewriter.*]

WARDEN [*watching her closely*]: Hope working nights don't interfere too much with your social life.

EVA [*tiredly*]: I don't have any social life right now.

WARDEN: How come?

EVA: I've been so busy job hunting since I moved here that I haven't had much time to cultivate friends.

WARDEN: No boyfriends, huh?

EVA: Oh, I have a few that I correspond with.

WARDEN: Yeah, but there's a limit to what can be put in an envelope, huh?

EVA: I suppose there is. —Mr. Whalen, there seem to be quite a number of bad discrepancies in the commissary report.

WARDEN: You mean it don't add up right?

EVA: I failed to account for about six hundred dollars.

[*The Warden whistles.*]

What shall I do about it?

WARDEN: I'll git Jim to check it over with you. You know a lot can be done about things like that by a little manipulation of figures. Jim'll explain that to you.

EVA: I see.

WARDEN: How long have you been working here?

EVA: Two weeks.

WARDEN: Gin'rally I git shut of a girl in less time'n that if she don't measure up to the job.

EVA [*tensely*]: I hope that I've shown my efficiency.

WARDEN: Aw, efficiency! I don't look for efficiency in my girls.

EVA: What do you look for, Mr. Whalen?

WARDEN: Personality! You're in a position where you got to meet the public. Big men politically come in this office—you give 'em a smile, they feel good—what do they care about the tax-payers' money? —Those boobs that go aroun' checkin' over accounts, where did this nickel go, what's done with that dime—jitney bums*, I call 'em! —No, Siree, I got no respect for a man that wants a job where he's got to make note of ev'ry red copper that happens to slip through his hands! —Well—policy, that's what I'm after! —Being political about certain matters, it don't hurt *ever*, yuh see?

EVA: Yes, I think so.

WARDEN [*pausing*]: What color's that blouse you got on?

EVA [*nervously sensing his approach*]: Chartreuse.

WARDEN [*half-extending his hand*]: It's right Frenchy-looking.

EVA: Thank you. [*She types rapidly.*]

WARDEN [*opening the inner door and coughing uncertainly*]: Look here.

EVA: Yes?

WARDEN: Why don't you drop that formality stuff? [*He crosses to her.*] How do I look to you? Unromantic? Not so much like one of the movie stars? —Well, it might surprise you to know how well I go over with some of the girls! [*He seats himself on corner of the desk.*] —I had a date not so long ago—girl works over at the Cattle and Grain Market—'bout your age, build, ev'rything— [*He licks his lips.*] —When I got through loving her up she says to me— "Do it again, Papa do

---

*Jitney: an adjective meaning "cheap."

it again!"— [*He roars with laughter and slaps the dock.*]
Why? Because she *loved* it, that why! [*He rises and goes to the
inner door.*] You ever been in here?

EVA: No.

WARDEN [*heartily*]: Come on in. I wanta show you how nice
I got it fixed up.

EVA: No.

WARDEN: Why not?

EVA [*rising stiffly*]: You're married, Mr. Whalen. I'm not that
kind of girl.

WARDEN: Aw, that act's been off the stage for years!

EVA: It's not an act, Mr. Whalen!

WARDEN: Naw, neither was *Uncle Tom's Cabin* when little
Eva goes up to heaven in Act III on a bunch of steel wires! [*He
slams the inner door angrily, then laughs.*] You're okay, sister.
You keep right on pitching in there.

EVA: Now that you know me better, do I still have a job?

WARDEN: Why, you betcha life you still got a job! [*He laughs
and grips her in a fumbling embrace which she rigidly endures.
Jim enters.*]

JIM: Excuse me.

WARDEN [*still laughing*]: Come on in, Jimmy boy. Want you
to check over this commissary report with Miss Crane. She says

there's a few—what you call 'em? Discrepancies! You know how to fix that up!

JIM: Yes, Sir.

WARDEN: How's things in Hall C? Pretty quiet?

JIM: Too quiet.

WARDEN: How's that?

JIM: When they make a noise you know what's going on.

WARDEN: They're scared to let a peep out since I put that bunch in the Hole.

JIM: I don't think so. I got an idea they might quit eating tonight.

WARDEN: Quit eating? You mean—*hunger strike*? [*The word scares him a little.*]

JIM: Yes. They're tired of spaghetti.

WARDEN: Maybe a change of climate would improve their appetites!

JIM: Klondike?

WARDEN: Yeah.

JIM: Klondike won't hold thirty-five hundred men.

WARDEN: It would hold Hall C.

JIM: Yes, but Butch is in Hall C.

WARDEN: What of it?

JIM: He's got a lot of influence with the men.

WARDEN: He's a troublemaker an' I'm gonna sweat it out of him.

JIM: I wouldn't try that, Boss. Hunger makes men pretty desperate and if you tortured them on top of that there's no telling what might happen.

WARDEN: Hunger strike's something I won't put up with in here. Creates a sensation all over the country. Then what? Cranks of ev'ry description start bitching about the brutal treatment of those goddamn mugs that would knife their own mothers for the price of a beer!

JIM: The easiest way to avoid it would be to improve the food.

WARDEN: Avoid it, hell. I'll bust it to pieces! Wait'll they see that gang we've got in the Hole—if that don't make sufficient impression I'll give 'em the heat! [*He leaves the office.*]

JIM: The man's a lunatic. Ask him who he is, he'd say, "Benito Mussolini!"

EVA: You're right about him. I suspected it last week when he made you show me those scars on your back. Just now—before you came in—he convinced me of it.

JIM: What happened?

EVA: He wanted me to go in that room with him.

JIM: You didn't?

EVA: No. I was sure he'd fire me but he only laughed and squeezed my arm— Look!

JIM: What?

EVA: I've got a blue mark on my arm where he pinched me.

JIM: When he was a boy I bet he got lots of fun drowning kittens and pulling the wings off butterflies. —Were you scared?

EVA: Terribly scared—and at the same time—something else.

JIM: What?

EVA: If I told you, you'd be disgusted with me.

JIM: Attracted?

EVA: Yes, in a way. I knew that if he touched me I wouldn't be able to move.

JIM: In the pulps they call it fascinated horror.

EVA: Yes. Or a horrible fascination.

JIM: So you're convinced it's no place for a lady?

EVA: I'm not going to quit. Not yet.

JIM: No? If you wait for a third alarm it might be too late.

EVA: I'm going to stay. I've got a favorite nightmare, Jim, about finding myself alone in a big empty house. And knowing that something or somebody was hidden behind one of the doors, waiting to grab me— But instead of running out of the house I always go searching through it; opening all of the closed doors— Even when I come to the last one, I don't stop, Jim—I open that one, too.

JIM: And what do you find?

EVA: I don't know. I always wake up just then.

JIM: So you're going to try the same thing here?

EVA: Something like that.

JIM: I guarantee you won't be disappointed. Gimme the commissary report— No, take that sheet out, we'll start over again— See how much spaghetti we can make out of a Packard Six.* Ten pounds of sodium fluoride. No, you better make it sixteen.

EVA: Sixteen pounds of sodium fluoride.

JIM: Sixteen pounds of—sodium fluoride.

EVA: You just gave me that.

JIM: Aw. Twenty bushels of—

EVA: Jim.

---

*The Packard was an American luxury car of the period.

JIM: Yeah?

EVA: Why don't you ever open the door *you're* hiding behind?

JIM: What makes you think I'm hiding behind anything?

EVA: Your eyes, the way your hands shake sometimes.

JIM: Oh. That.

EVA: It would help to let go. I mean with the right person.

JIM: Who is that right person?

EVA: Me.

JIM: How do I know?

EVA: Because I tell you.

JIM: Lots of people tell lots of things and most of them are lies.

EVA: I'm not lying, Jim—I want you to trust me.

JIM: Okay.

EVA: Then tell me—what is it?

JIM: What?

EVA: Your hands—why do they shake like this?

JIM: I thought I gave you a clear demonstration once.

EVA: When?

JIM: That morning we heard the band music.

EVA: You mean it's—repression.

JIM: That's it. Something that's locked up and keeps getting more and more all the time. There's lots of men in here with fingers that shake like this. It's power. Outside it runs dynamos, lights up big cities. But in here the power's all gone to waste. It just feeds on itself, gets bigger, does nothing. Till something sets it off like a match does a keg of powder—and then you got an explosion!

EVA: Explosions are such a—waste—of power!

JIM: Yeah. But what's the alternative here?

EVA: Your writing!

JIM: Editorials for *The Archaeopteryx*?

EVA: No! You've got next month to think of, Jim.

JIM: Next month is still on the lap of the gods. Which is a complimentary way of referring to the Board of Pardons and Paroles.

EVA: I don't know why, but I feel so sure of it, Jim. These ten years of—of waiting— They've made you stronger than other men are— You've stored up so much in you that when you get it out, there's nothing could stand in your way— You'll push down all the ordinary walls and walk right over them, Jim— People will say, "Who is this man? Where did he come from?"—and I'll smile proudly because I'll know. —He's a man from another country, I'll say— He's a giant— He's got lightning in his right hand and thunder in his left— But I'll know— I'll know secrets about you—all the sweet, strange things that only a woman can know—and I can tell you— [*Whalen enters.*] How many pounds was that—of sodium fluoride?

JIM: Sixteen.

WARDEN: How you getting along with that report?

JIM: We haven't done much yet. We got to talking.

WARDEN: About what?

JIM: Fireworks.

WARDEN: Very appropriate. Schulz is bringing the Hole gang up for inspection. Get them chairs out of the way.

JIM: Yes, Sir.

WARDEN: You stand over by the window and look sharp! Eva—you wanta stay in here or go in the next room?

EVA: I'll stay.

[*A buzzer sounds.*]

WARDEN: Okay. March 'em in! [*A file of haggard, ghostly figures shuffles into the room, their eyes blinking against the light, barely able to stand—some with heads bloody, others with clotted, shredded shirts. The Warden whistles.*]

SCHULTZ: Stand up against that wall!

WARDEN: Nice-lookin' bunch. Oughta make quite an impression when they go back to Hall C! [*To Swifty*]: How long have you been in the hole, Son?

[*Swifty cannot speak. His lips move and he staggers forward with a pleading gesture. The Warden raises the "billy" and continues.*]

Stand back there! Why don't you speak?

JIM: He can't talk.

WARDEN: Dumb?

EVA: No. Sick. He's had five days in a strait jacket.

WARDEN: I think he needs five more.

[*Swiftly falls to his knees.*]

JIM: I think Swifty's had enough, boss.

WARDEN: Who asked you?

JIM: Nobody.

WARDEN: Just volunteered the information?

JIM: Yes, Sir.

WARDEN: Maybe you'd like to take his place down there?

JIM: No, Sir.

WARDEN: Then you'd better cut the cackle. Ollie?

OLLIE [*faintly*]: Yes, Sir.

WARDEN: You look kind of all in.

OLLIE [*his voice shaking*]: I is, suh. I neahly checked out las' night. Boss, ah didn' think ad'd live t' see day!

WARDEN: Think another night would just about fix you up?

OLLIE: Couldn't make it, Boss.

WARDEN: What do you think, Schultz?

SCHULTZ: I think another night would do that boy a world of good, Mr. Whalen.

OLLIE [*wildly*]: Please, God, Boss, ah cain't make it! Ah cain't *make* it!

WARDEN: Two nights! —One extra for squawking!

OLLIE: Oh, Laws, a mussy, please, oh, Jesus, please, a mussy— [*He continues this prayer in a sort of chant as they are led out the door.*]

WARDEN: Get 'em out! I'll check 'em over again tomorrow morning.

[*They shuffle out slowly, Ollie chanting his prayer. Jim follows.*]

Ever heard such a squawk?

[*Eva sinks wearily into a chair.*]

You going to flip out again?

EVA: No. I'm all right. They looked so awful it made me a little sick.

WARDEN: Sure they looked awful. Maybe they'll appreciate good treatment after this—I'll wager there'll be no more kick about food.

[*From the hall comes the sound of a disturbance—Jim enters.*]

WARDEN: What's going on out there?

JIM: Ollie just—

WARDEN: Took a dive?

JIM: Yes. Butted his head against a wall and broke it.

WARDEN: Head or wall?

JIM: Head.

WARDEN: All right. Cart him over to the sick-house.

JIM: Not the sick-house.

WARDEN: Dead?

JIM: Yes.

WARDEN: Why dontcha watch out? You coulda prevented that— Give Eva one of them cards— Naw, outa the top drawer. Fill that out. Name— What was that smoke's name?

JIM: Oliver. Oliver Jackson.

WARDEN: Special friend of yours?

JIM: All of the men liked Ollie.

WARDEN: Huh. How old?

JIM: Twenty-six.

WARDEN: Color—black! Sentence—

JIM: Three years.

WARDEN: Charge?

JIM [*slowly*]: Stole a crate of canned goods off a truck to feed his family.

WARDEN: Larceny! —Cause of death? —What's his Wasserman?

JIM: Negative.

WARDEN: Hmmm. Put this down, Eva. Stomach Ulcers. Severe hemorrhages.

JIM: That's what you gave the boy last week.

WARDEN: Well, make it a bad cold—complications—pneumonia!

[*The sounds of yammering begin to penetrate the office.*]

[*The Warden is unnerved for a moment but continues.*] What's that?

JIM: They're making a noise.

WARDEN [*instinctively seizing his whip*]: Where's it from? Hall C?

JIM: Naw. Halls A, B, C, D, E, and F!

WARDEN [*shakily*]: What are they bitching about now?

JIM: They must have heard about Ollie. They like him pretty good.

WARDEN: Aw— [*He looks frightened.*] —Schultz! [*He seizes the phone.*] Schultz? How's the pipes in Klondike? Git them radiators tested an' ready for action.

[*There is a sudden complete darkness on stage.*]

WHISPERS [*gradually rising in volume and pitch*]: Somebody got hurt downstairs— Who was it? —Ollie! —Ollie? —Yeah, they killed Ollie —Ollie's dead. —They killed Ollie— Ollie's dead— They KILLED OLLIE— THEY KILLED OLLIE— OLLIE'S DEAD!

[*A spot comes up on the cell. Butch is bending to the wall. He suddenly rises.*]

BUTCH: Ollie's dead— THEY KILLED OLLIE! [*He shouts through the bars.*]

CHORUS: Ollie's dead! They killed Ollie!

JOE: What are we going to do about it?

BUTCH: Quit eating! [*He shouts through the bars*] QUIT EATING!

CHORUS: Quit eating! Quit eating!

[*Blackout.*]

WHISPERS: What does Butch say? —Butch says quit eating— hunger strike? —Yeah, hunger strike! —Butch says HUNGER STRIKE! —Hunger strike—quit eating— Quit eating— HUNGER STRIKE!

VOICE: The men in Hall C have quit eating!

SECOND VOICE: Hunger strike in Hall C!

NEWSBOY: *Morning Star*! Paper! *Morning Star*! Paper! Read about the big hunger strike!

WOMAN'S VOICE: It is reported that some of the men in the state prison have gone on a hunger strike!

[*The click of a telegraph is heard.*]

VOICE: Associated Press Bulletin— Hunger strike at Monroe City Penitentiary! Men rebel against monotonous diet!

VOICE: United Press!

VOICE: Columbia Broadcasting System!

VOICE: Commissioners promise an investigation of alleged starvation in state penitentiary!

VOICE: Warden denies hunger strike!

VOICE: Hunger strike reported!

VOICE: Hunger strike denied!

VOICE: Hunger strike! HUNGER STRIKE!

[*Traffic noises, sirens, bells are heard. Theme up: "1812 Overture" theme reprise. Blackout. Fade.*]

END OF ACT ONE

ACT TWO

Announcer: "Not About Nightingales!"

A spot comes up on the office. The hunger strike has been in effect for several days and a tense, electric atmosphere prevails as everyone waits for the inevitable explosion when nerves are stretched beyond the point of endurance. Eva is seated alone as the scene opens. Her movements are jittery. The phone rings.

EVA: Warden's office. *The Morning Star?* No, Mr. Whalen is not seeing any reporters. No, there is no serious trouble. No, you can't get on the Island without a special permit from Mr. Whalen. The rule has been in effect for about six days. No, not on account of a hunger strike! Yes, good-bye.

[*During this the Chaplain has entered. Eva is startled, then continues.*]

Oh!

CHAPLAIN: Nervous, young lady?

EVA: Terribly—terribly!

CHAPLAIN: I don't blame you. So am I. This thing has got to be stopped before something serious happens.

EVA: Oh, if it only could be!

CHAPLAIN: That's what I want to see Mr. Whalen about. It does no good trying to suppress all news of what's going on. We might as well face the music—and do something constructive to put a stop to it!

EVA: Yes. Something constructive.

CHAPLAIN: But in the meantime—couldn't you take a little vacation?

EVA: You think there's real—danger?

CHAPLAIN: Certainly there's danger. And it's aggravated by the fact that Mr. Whalen apparently won't recognize it. I wish that I could reason with that man, but— Well— [*He glances at his watch.*] —I'll visit some boys in the hospital and be back here for a talk with the Boss in about twenty minutes.

EVA: All right.

[*Jim enters.*]

CHAPLAIN: Hello, Jim. How are things upstairs?

JIM [*showing a bloody arm in a torn sleeve*]: That's the answer!

EVA [*springing up*]: Jim!

JIM [*laughing grimly*]: I walked too close to one of the cages.

CHAPLAIN: Who did that?

JIM [*slowly shaking his head*]: I don't know.

CHAPLAIN [*patting his back*]: You've had ten bad years, Jim. I hope next month will be the end of it for you.

JIM: Thanks, Reverend. [*The Chaplain goes out.*]

EVA: Jim, I'll—I'll fix that up for you.

[*He sits down by desk.*]

JIM: They gave me this stuff to put on it down at the sick-house. They were sore as hell because I wouldn't tell them who done it.

EVA [*painting his arm and applying a bandage*]: You should-n't stay up there. It's not safe for you.

JIM: No place is safe in here. Aren't you finally convinced of that?

EVA: Why are you so anxious to get rid of me?

JIM: You know a lot you could tell.

EVA: Yes. I suppose I do.

JIM: Why don't you then?

EVA: I want to stay here a while longer. Maybe next month I'll go—we'll both go then.

JIM: They've been on a hunger strike six days and the Warden only gave them seven. Tonight may be the deadline. To-morrow night at the latest.

EVA: Then what?

JIM: The boiler room is in perfect condition. The pipes have been reinforced.

EVA: I can't imagine anything as brutal as that—I don't believe it!

JIM: Well—I ought to spill it myself—but if I did it would cost my ticket-of-leave!— It's funny.

EVA: What?

JIM: Nothing has quite so much value as the skin our own guts are wrapped in. [*He takes a book and sits down at the window.*]

[*Eva resumes typing. Jim suddenly tears a page out and throws it on the floor in disgust.*]

Christ!

EVA: What did you do that for?

JIM: I didn't like it.

EVA: What was it?

JIM: A little piece of verbal embroidery by a guy named Keats.

EVA: What's wrong with it?

JIM: It's sissy stuff—"Ode to a Nightingale!" Don't those literary punks know there's something more important to write about than that? They ought to spend a few years in stir before they select their subjects!

EVA: Why don't you show them, then?

JIM: I'd give my right arm for the chance.

EVA: You have the chance!

JIM: Not in here I don't. If I wrote what I wanted to write, I'd stay in here till Klondike becomes an ice-plant! —But maybe next month—

EVA: Yes. Next month—

JIM: Maybe then I'll start writing—but not about nightingales!

EVA: John Keats didn't have a very good time of it, Jim.

JIM: No?

EVA: No. He died at the age of twenty-six.

JIM: Smothered himself in lilies, I guess.

EVA: No. He wanted to live. Terribly. He was like you, he had a lot of things he wanted to say but no chance to say them. He wrote another poem, Jim. A poem you'd like. Give me the book—here it is! [*She reads the sonnet "When I have fears that I may cease to be"*]:

> When I have fears that I may cease to be
> Before my pen has gleaned my teeming brain,
> Before high piléd books, in charactry,
> Hold like rich garners the full-ripened grain;
> When I behold, upon the night's starred face,
> Huge cloudy symbols of high romance,
> And think that I may never live to trace

> Their shadows, with the magic hand of chance;
> And when I feel, fair creature of an hour!
> That I shall never look upon thee more,
> Never have relish in the faery power
> Of unreflecting love! —then on the shore
> Of the wide world I stand alone, and think
> Till Love and Fame to nothingness do sink.

You see he was like you, Jim. He got out of his prison by looking at the stars. He wrote about beauty as a form of escape.

JIM: Escape, huh? That's not my kind of escape.

EVA: What is your form of escape?

JIM: Blowing things wide open!

EVA: Destruction, you mean?

JIM: Yes! Destruction!

EVA: I'm sorry to hear you say that.

JIM: Would you rather hear me warbling about nightingales?

EVA: No. But there are other things.

JIM: For instance?

EVA: There must be some things you love.

JIM: Love?

EVA: Yes.

JIM: Love is something nasty that's done in dark corners around this place.

EVA: I'm sorry you're so bitter.

JIM: Why should you be sorry about anything except the possible loss of your job?

EVA: Why should I? Because I like you, Jim.

JIM: Even after—after the last time we were in here together?

EVA: More than ever.

JIM: When you've been without women as long as I have, there's something mythological about them. You can't believe they're real, not even when you place your hands on them like this and—

EVA: Jim! [*She breaks away as Whalen enters.*]

WARDEN: What's the matter Jim?

JIM: Why?

WARDEN: You got a funny look on your face.

JIM: I'm just concentrating.

WARDEN: On what?

JIM: The new *Archaeopteryx*.

WARDEN: Aw, what are you going to write about, Jim?

JIM [*quietly*]: Not about—nightingales.

WARDEN: Huh? [*Absently fiddles with his papers.*] Aw, Jim—

JIM: Yes, Sir?

WARDEN: You might want to drop a word to the boys on hunger strike about the radiator test we made in Klondike. We got the temperature up to 150 degrees— You might mention that. You know a word to the wise is sufficient.

JIM: I'm afraid there's not much wisdom in Hall C. Good night.

[*Jim goes out. The Chaplain enters.*]

WARDEN [*lighting cigar*]: What do yuh want, Reverend?

CHAPLAIN: I want to talk to you about the death of Oliver Jackson.

WARDEN: What about it?

CHAPLAIN: I think it could have been avoided.

WARDEN: Sure it could. Nobody made that fool nigger take a dive.

CHAPLAIN: He was goaded to desperation.

WARDEN: Oh, you think so?

CHAPLAIN: There have been too many suicides, several drownings, hangings, so-called accidents, since I've been here.

Now it appears that we're in danger of having a mass suicide in Hall C. The men have gone on hunger strike which I think is fully justified by the quality of food they've been getting.

WARDEN: Aw. Now I'm beginning to suspect who's responsible for the wild stories that have been leaking out to the public about things here. I'm afraid you're what the boys call a— stool pigeon, Reverend.

CHAPLAIN: I'm a conscientious steward of Christ, and as such I protest against the inhuman treatment of convicts in this prison!

WARDEN [jumping up]: Who's running this prison, you or me?

CHAPLAIN: Mr. Whalen, the universe is like a set of blocks. The kind you had in kindergarten. A little one that fits into a big one, a bigger one over that, till you get on up to the very biggest of them all that fits on top of all the rest—

WARDEN: Yes?

CHAPLAIN: Yes, and that biggest block is the one I'm representing—the Kingdom of God. [He rises with dignity.]

WARDEN: Well, I'm afraid your work here has begun to interfere with your—your higher duties— I want you to climb up there on top of that great big block you're talkin' about an' stay up there. That's your place. You leave me alone down here on the little block— There's your notice, Reverend— You're free to go now.

CHAPLAIN: I could leave here gladly if it wasn't for what I have to take with me.

WARDEN: You're taking nothing with you but the clothes on your back.

CHAPLAIN: I'm taking much more than that.

WARDEN: Aw. Maybe I'd better have you frisked on the way out.

CHAPLAIN: You could strip me naked and I'd still have these.

WARDEN: These what?

CHAPLAIN: Memories—shadows—ghosts!

WARDEN: Ahhhh? [*He lifts phone.*] Git me Atwater 2770.

CHAPLAIN: Things I've seen that I can't forget. Men, tortured, twisted, driven mad. Death's the least of it. It's the *life* in here that's going to stay with me like an incurable sickness. And by God, Whalen, that's not profanity—by God, I won't rest easy till I've seen these walls torn down, stone by stone, and others put up in their place that let the air in! Good night!— [*He goes out quickly.*]

WARDEN: Hello. Reverend? This is Warden Whalen. Our chaplain's just resigned. I want you to come over and talk to me—might be a steady job in it for you. Yes, Siree! You be over here in time for Sunday service— [*He hangs up.*] Memories, shadows, ghosts! What a screwball! [*He pours himself a drink.*]

DIM OUT

Announcer: "Sunday Morning in Hall C!"

A spot comes up on the cell. Joe, Queen, and Swifty are reading sections of a Sunday paper. From down the corridor comes Butch's voice—

BUTCH [*approaching*]: "I'm forever BLOW-ing BUB-BLES!" [*He enters the cell with a straight razor, towel, and soap.*] Who gave you that paper?

JOE: Allison. The Canary.

BUTCH: Git it out of here!

JOE: What for?

BUTCH: It's contaminated.

JOE: Aw, take a look at t' comics.

BUTCH: Naw, gimme 'at pitcher section. Hey! Look at 'is!

JOE: What?

BUTCH: "A bow-ket of buds!"

JOE: Yeah. They're comin' out in sassiety.

BUTCH: "Miss Hortense Maxine Schultz, daughter of Mr. and Mrs. Max W. Schultz, 79 Willow Drive, will make her bow to society early this Fall. She is one of a group of young women who traveled through Europe this summer with Mrs. J. Mortimer Finchwell—"

JOE: So what?

BUTCH: "On her fadder's side Miss Schultz is directly descendant from William th' Conq'ror an' on her mudders from Ponce de Leon, Sir Isaac Newton an' George Washington's Aunt!"

JOE: Gosh, de're pikers! Why don't they throw in Benito Mussolini for good measure?

BUTCH: "Her grandfather was duh late Benjamin F. Schultz, President and founder of th' Shultz Bottling Works."

JOE: Lotsa mazooma, huh?

BUTCH: "In addition to her many udder accomplishments—!" Hey, listen to this!

JOE: Huh?

BUTCH: Down here at th' bottom they come right out an' admit that she ain't even human!

JOE: How's that?

BUTCH: It says here "In addition to her many udder accomplishments, Miss Schultz is an excellent *horse*-woman!"

JOE: Hell, you could tell that by lookin' at her pitcher.*

BLACKOUT

---

*A Hunt Club was prestigious in St. Louis in 1936 when the *Post Dispatch* reported 1000 persons attending the Spring Horse Show. "Schultz Bottling Works" is doubtless the Anheuser Busch brewery. In this scene Williams satirizes St. Louis society, from which his family was excluded, as being dominated by *nouveau riche* beer barons.

EPISODE THREE

Announcer: "Mr. Whalen Interviews the New Chaplain!"

A spot comes up on the office. Whalen and the Reverend Hooker have just returned from Sunday dinner. The Reverend Hooker is a nervous, precise little man with a prodigious anxiety to please.

WARDEN: I got you up here on pretty short notice. You see me an' the old chaplain had a little disagreement last night, which resulted in him handing in his resignation right off the bat! — He made one fatal mistake, Reverend— He kind of forgot who was in charge of this institution.

REVEREND: I don't think I shall make that error, Mr. Whalen.

WARDEN: Naw, neither do I. First time I seen you I said to myself "Here's a man who looks like he could adjust himself to conditions."

REVEREND: I pride myself on being—adjustable!

WARDEN: Good. You'll find that's an asset around this place, a definite asset. What's your idea of the universe, Reverend?

REVEREND: I beg your pardon?

WARDEN: Suppose you give me a little word-picture of how you conceive of this great mysterious— [*He makes a sweeping gesture.*]

REVEREND: Cosmos?

WARDEN: Yes! In which we humans are little fluttering motes, so to speak. [*He makes a derisive fluttering gesture with hands.*]

REVEREND: Well—uh—of course there's the orthodox conception of the universe as consisting of three elements—

WARDEN: Yep?

REVEREND: Heaven, earth and the—uh—regions below.

WARDEN: We call that Klondike in here.

REVEREND: I beg your pardon?

WARDEN: Skip it, Reverend.

REVEREND: Hmmm. Of course there is some question as to the *material* existence of those—uh—nether regions—

WARDEN: There's no doubt about 'em here. Naw, Sir. But what I wanted to know, Reverend, is if you've got any theories about a set of blocks—with you occupying the one on top and me way down at the bottom—that's what got the last preacher in trouble with me.

REVEREND: Blocks? Oh, dear, no! That strikes me as rather—elementary to say the least!

WARDEN: Yeah, kindergarten stuff. Well, you'll do, Reverend. [*He glances at his ponderous gold watch.*] We got about five minutes till church takes up. Are you good at makin' up extemporaneous speeches?

REVEREND: Oh, yes, indeed, yes, indeed! I think I may safely say that I have never lacked words for any occasion, Mr. Whalen.

WARDEN: Well, your job depends on this one. I haven't got time to go into details, Reverend. But I want you to touch on three particular subjects. I don't care how you bring 'em in, just so you *do* and so you give 'em the right emphasis!

REVEREND: Three subjects!

WARDEN: Yes, Siree. You mark 'em down, Reverend—food!

REVEREND: Food?

WARDEN: That's the first one. Then—heat!

REVEREND: Heat?

WARDEN: Yep. And then—Klondike! [*A bell sounds.*] There goes the bell. I'm two minutes slow. Remember, now, food, heat, and Klondike!

REVEREND: What was the last one? Klondike? You mean— uh—missionary work in the far north? Among the Eskimos? I'm afraid the association of ideas is going to be a little difficult for me to grasp, Mr. Whalen—but—

[*Dim out; a spot comes up on the Reverend Hooker behind a small lectern.*]

REVEREND: Yes—uh—very good afternoon to you all. [*He clears his throat: then beams at the convicts.*] I hope that you enjoyed your dinner as much as I did mine—

VOICE: Hamburgers and spaghetti! [*There is a chorus of booing. A warning whistle sounds, then silence.*]

REVEREND: Food is such a familiar blessing that—uh we sometimes forget to be properly grateful for it. But when I read about the horrible conditions in famine-stricken portions of Europe and Asia—tch, tch!—I feel that I am indeed very fortunate to have a full stomach!

[*Booing is heard; someone whistles.*]

When one thinks of food—uh—one also thinks by a natural association of ideas—about—uh—the marvelous blessing of—uh—*Heat*! Heat—uh—that makes food possible—wonderful *heat*! Heat of all kinds! The heat of the sun that warms the earth's atmosphere and permits the growth of the vegetables and the grains and the—uh—fruits—uh—the heat of the—uh—body—uh— [*He wipes his forehead.*] heat, universal heat— At this time of the year some of us find heat oppressive—uh—but that is ungrateful of us, extremely ungrateful—

[*There is a slow stomping of feet.*]

[*The preacher continues, raising his voice.*] For all living matter depends on the presence of heat—northward and southward from the Equator to the twin poles—even to far Alaska—even in *Klondike*—

[*The stomping grows louder.*]

What would Klondike be without heat? A frozen wasteland! [*He scrubs his forehead and glances nervously about.*] In Klondike our brave missionaries, risking their lives among savage tribes of war—painted Indians—

[*A hymnal is hurled: there is furious stomping.*]

Goodness! —As I was saying—in Klondike—!

[*He is bombarded with hymnals. A whistle blows; there is shouting; a siren sounds. Dim out. A mocking jazz interlude plays. A spot comes up on the office. The Reverend rushes in clasping his handkerchief to his forehead.*]

REVEREND: Oh, mercy upon us!

WARDEN [*at the phone*]: Schultz? All guards on duty! Find out who conked the Reverend with that song book. Whew! I give you my word, Reverend, I wasn't expecting no such a reaction as this! It come as a complete surprise!

REVEREND: Ohhhh! I'm afraid I shall have to receive some medical attention.

WARDEN: Yeah, well, I want you to take this fin, Reverend.

REVEREND: And the nervous shock, you know! Tch, Tch!

WARDEN: Yeah? Well—

REVEREND: Terrific, terrific! A shocking experience!

WARDEN: Here's another two bucks.

[*Theme up: jazz*]

BLACKOUT

EPISODE FOUR

Announcer: "Zero Hour!"

A spot comes up on the warden's office. Eva is typing nervously. Jim enters. His chronic tension has now risen to the point of breaking. Even his movements are stiff like those of a mechanical man: his eyes are smoldering.

EVA [*jumping up as he enters*]: Jim, you're not—?

JIM: Naw, I'm not locked up in Hall C.

EVA: I hadn't seen you. I was afraid—

JIM: You must have forgotten what a special value there is attached to my hide.

EVA: You look awfully tired, Jim.

JIM: Yes. How do *you* sleep at night?

EVA: Not well lately.

JIM: How do you sleep at all knowing what you know and keeping still?

EVA: What else can I do but keep still?

JIM: You could talk. You could tell the State Humane Society that thirty-five hundred animals are being starved to death and threatened with torture.

EVA: And lose my job?

JIM: Aw. Excuse me for being so impractical.

EVA: You don't understand. I was out of work six months before I got this job.

JIM: You told me that.

EVA: I got down to my last dime. Once a man followed along the street and I stood still, waiting for him to catch up with me. Yes, I'd gotten down that low, I was going to ask him for money—

JIM: Did you?

EVA: No. At the last moment I couldn't. I went hungry instead.

[*Jim looks at her.*]

Now you want me to go back to that? Times haven't improved. Now maybe I'd have more courage, or less decency, or maybe I'd be hungrier than I was before.

JIM: You'd better hold on to your job, Miss Crane—even if it does mean participating in a massacre!

EVA: It's not that bad.

JIM: It's going to be that bad. I'm going to talk myself now. Even if it means giving up my chance of parole.

EVA: No, you can't do that. Wait a while and see how things turn out.

JIM: This is the zero hour. Whalen has given instructions to put Hall C in Klondike tonight If they don't eat supper.

EVA: I know. I heard him.

[*Jim lifts the telephone receiver*]

What are you going to do?

JIM: Blow the lid off this stinking hole!

EVA [*grabbing the phone*]: No, Jim! I'll do it, myself! I'll talk!

JIM: When?

EVA [*lowering her voice*]: Now. Tonight. I'll visit the newspaper on my way home.

JIM: You will, huh?

EVA: Yes!

JIM: No. Wait till tomorrow. We'll have more definite evidence then. With Hall C in Klondike.

[*Whalen enters.*]

WARDENS: Well, Jim. What do the boys in Hall C think about the change in climate that I've arranged for them?

JIM: They haven't heard yet. Wilson is going to tell them when he brings the men up from the Hole.

WARDEN: They'll be eating supper tonight.

JIM: What have they got for supper?

WARDEN: The old perennial favorites, hamburger and spaghetti. I'm not going to mollycoddle those bastards. —Excuse me, Eva.

JIM: I don't think they'll eat.

WARDEN: You don't, huh? Well, I do! Eva—

EVA [*who has gotten her hat*]: Yes, Sir?

WARDEN: I'll want you back after supper. We've got to have things in perfect order in case the snoopers get busy.

EVA: All right.

WARDEN: You'd better catch the ferry at seven-fifteen.

EVA: Yes, Sir. [*She exits.*]

JIM: About my parole, Mr. Whalen—

WARDEN: Yes? What about it?

JIM: It's coming up next month.

WARDEN [*grunting*]: Humph.

JIM: I guess it pretty much hangs on your decision.

WARDEN: You've got a lot of brass.

JIM: Why do you say that?

WARDEN: Bothering me about your goddamn parole at a time like this!

JIM: It's important to me. I've been in here ten years and I've got ten years of copper. I'm due for a ticket-of-leave.

WARDEN: You'll get a ticket to Klondike if you got any more to say on that subject!

JIM [*starting forward*]: By God, I—

WARDEN: What?

JIM [*with desperate control*]: Nothing.

WARDEN [*uneasily*]: I'm going out for supper. Be back about eight or eight-thirty. You watch things here.

JIM: Yes, Sir.

[*Whalen exits. Jim covers his face, strangling a sob.*]

BLACKOUT

Musical theme up: "I'm Forever Blowing Bubbles."

Announcer:"Hall C!" Musical theme fade.

A spot comes up on the cell. The dialogue is fairly light, but an undercurrent of desperation should be felt.

BUTCH [*hoarsely*]: "I'm forever blow-ing BUBBLES!"

JOE: Quit croakin' that corny number. Why dontcha learn something new?

BUTCH: That was new last I heard it.

JOE: Before you got in stir?

BUTCH: It had just come out.

JOE: It's had time to grow whiskers since then.

BUTCH: It was Goldie's fav'rite.

JOE: I thought you said she liked *Dardanella*.

BUTCH: She liked that one, too.

JOE: What's become of her?

BUTCH: How should I know? She quit writing ten years ago.

JOE: Christ. She's probably died of the syph by now.

BUTCH: Naw, not Goldie.

QUEEN: I wish I was dead. I used to have nice fingernails. Look at 'em now. My teeth was nice, too. I had nice hair. Now when I look at myself I wish I was dead.

BUTCH: "Faw'chun's always hi-ding! I looked ev'ry where!"

[*A mimic down the hall echoes the refrain.*]

BUTCH [*jumping to the bars*]: Who was that? You, Krause? —Anytime I want you small-time grifters to muscle in on my singin' I'll send you a special request.

QUEEN: Yes, I wish I was dead. I hope that I starve to death. And I will. I can feel myself dying already.

BUTCH: "They fly so high, nearly reach the sky—" They used to turn out the light on that number. There was a sort of silver glass ball at the top of the ceilin' that would turn round and round an' throw little rainbow-colored reflections all over the floor an' the walls— God, it was lovely!

QUEEN [*rising*]: Honest to God, I can't hold out much longer, Butch!

BUTCH: Naw?

QUEEN: Naw, I got a weak constitution. I was in a nervous run-down condition before I got sent up here. Hell, it was a bum rap. I didn't sell any weeds. I used to smoke 'em but I never sold any! —Persecution, all my life, persecution! Now maybe they'll kill me down there in Klondike, I'll never git out, never—never git out!

BUTCH: Dummy up!

QUEEN: You ever been in Klondike, Joe?

JOE: Naw. Butch has.

QUEEN: What's it like, Butch?

BUTCH [*rising slowly and going to stage front*]: "Then like my dreams they fade an' die—"

QUEEN: They say it ain't the heat so much.

JOE: What is it? The humidity?

QUEEN: Naw, you can't breathe good. It's kind of—suffocating! [*He fingers his collar.*]

BUTCH: Fortune's always hiding—I looked ev'rywhere! I'm forever blow-ing BUBBLES! [*He stops short.*]

[*A door clangs—the men rise simultaneously, tense. There is the sound of a wracking cough and delirious sobbing.*]

[*Butch continues softly.*] They're bringin' 'em up from the Hole.

SCHULTZ: Gwan, git a move on, it ain't no funeral march yet awhile!

[*The dull shuffling of feet is heard accompanied by coughing, sobbing. The heads of the men in the cells move slowly from left to right, mouths open, as though watching some awful procession.*]

Halt! Face your cells! —You, too, Shapiro, do I have to speak Yiddish to make you understand?

[*A low yammering commences. Butch seizes his tin cup and holds it poised. A whistle sounds; the cell door opens.*]

March in! Git in there, Trout—Shapiro!

[*Swifty stumbles into the cell, unshaven, ghastly, sobbing.*]

Awright! Take a good look at 'em. An' remember this! The Hole is just a small dose compared to Klondike! Klondike's the big medicine and the Boss is all set to pour it out in double doses for any of you wise bastards that don't feel like eating supper tonight!

VOICE [*slowly and emphatically*]: Where's Ollie?

ANOTHER [*staccato*]: Yeah, where's Ollie?

CHORUS: Where's Ollie, where's Ollie, what did you do with Ollie?

[*Slight pause.*]

SCHULTZ: Who's responsible if some fool nigger takes a notion to butt his own brains out? [*There is a slight whine of fear in his voice.*]

[*Butch suddenly hammers the cell bar with his cup. Yammering commences. During the preceding speeches, from the point of his entrance, Swifty has stood dazed; then he sags slowly to his knees beside the bunk. The Queen comforts him awkwardly. Joe and Butch stand with attention fixed on Schultz. A whistle sounds. The yammering subsides a little.*]

[*Schultz, standing directly outside the open cell door, continues*]: You see this here thermometer? [*He extracts a large one from his pocket.*] See that little red mark there? That says Blood Heat. Now see this one up here twenty degrees more? It says Fever Heat. You think it's going to stop there? Not a chance! It's going to keep right on rising till it busts clean out of the top of the little doojigit! It's going to break all records. It's going to be the biggest heat wave in history. Now if you don't think I'm a good weather prophet, just one of you finicky lads leave a little spaghetti on his plate tonight an' see what happens!

VOICE: Spaghetti?

[*There is complete tense silence for a moment.*]

SCHULTZ: Yeah, spaghetti!

BUTCH: Spaghetti, huh? —We ain't gonna eat it tonight or no other time—not till Whalen cuts out the graft and feeds us something besides hog-slop!

SCHULTZ: Is 'at what you want me to tell him?

BUTCH: Yeah, tell him that, an' if he don't like it—

[*Yammering; a whistle; the door clangs shut; the yammering subsides.*]

VOICE: Klondike?

ANOTHER: Tonight?

ANOTHER: Yeah, if we don't eat!

VOICE: Klondike? No?

ANOTHER: Not if we go to Klondike!

VOICE [*shrill and despairing*]: We can't make it!!

[*A wracking cough and delirious sobbing are heard. Mex prays in a hoarse strangled voice.*]

MEX: *Santa María—Madre de Dios—* etc.

[*Butch advances to the bars and raps commandingly.*]

VOICE: It's Butch!

ANOTHER: What does Butch say?

MEX: *Jésus—muerto por nuestros pecados!*

BUTCH: Cut the cackle all of yuz! That goes for you too, Mex. You got plenty of time for talking to Jesus when you git there! Lissen here now! —Anybody in Hall C that eats is gonna pay for his supper in Kangaroo Court. I'll assess the maximum fine, you know what! —You're scared of Klondike? I say let 'em throw us in Klondike! —Maybe some of you weak sisters will be melted down to grease-chunks. But not all twenty-five of us! Some of us are gonna beat Klondike! And Klondike's dere las' trump card, when you got that licked, you've licked everything they've got to offer in here! You got 'em over the barrel for good! So then what happens? They come up to us and they say, "You win! What is it you want?" We say, "Boss Whalen is out! Git us a new Warden! Git us decent livin' conditions! No more overcrowdin', no more bunkin' up wit' contajus diseasus; fresh air in the cell-blocks, fumigation, an' most of all —WE WANT SOME FOOD THAT'S FIT TO PUT IN OUR BELLIES! [*Applause.*] No more hamburger an' spaghetti an' beans, and beans an' hamburger an' spaghetti till you feel like the whole fucking world was made of nothin' else but hamburger an' beans an' spaghetti— [*Applause.*] —Maybe when we git through house-cleaning this place'll be like the Industrial Reformatory they got at Chillicothe! A place where guys are learnt how to make a livin' after they git outa stir! Where they teach 'em trades an' improve their ejication! Not just lock 'em up in dirty holes an' hope to God they'll die so as to save the State some money!! [*Fierce yammering.*] Tonight we go to Klondike! —Dere's three compartments! One of 'em's little hell, one of 'em's middle-sized hell an' one of 'em's BIG HELL! —You know which one Butch O'Fallon is gonna be in! —So if I ain't yellow, boys, don't you be neither! That's all I got to say.

VOICE: Okay, Butch.

ANOTHER: We're witcha!

CHORUS: We'll beat Klondike! —You bet we'll beat it! —Put Whalen over a barrel— [*There is nervous laughter and applause.*]

[*Their voices die abruptly under a shadow of fear.*]

MEX [*chanting*]: *Muerto—por nuestros pecados—rojo—de sangre es—el Sol!*

BLACKOUT

Announcer: "Definition of Life!"

A spot comes up on the office. Jim, facing downstage, leans against the desk, smoking. Eva enters.

EVA: Hello, Jim.

JIM: Yeah.

EVA: Nice out. A little bit cooler. —What's wrong with you?

JIM [*grinning wryly*]: Ask me what life is, Eva.

[*Eva looks at him and crosses downstage.*]

Ask me what it is and I'll tell you.

EVA [*removing her hat*]: No, darling.

JIM: Why not?

EVA: It smells like a bad epigram.

JIM [*tossing away his cigarette*]: It's a gradual process of dying, that's what it is!

EVA: Worse than I expected.

JIM: That's what it is in here. Maybe it's something else on your side of the fence. I'd like to find out, but I guess I won't have the chance!

EVA [*seriously*]: Your parole?

[*Jim strikes a match, watches it burn.*]

Turned down?

JIM: Not yet but it will be. I was talking about it to Whalen.

EVA: Oh. You shouldn't have mentioned it now when he's all steamed up about the hunger strike.

JIM: I didn't mean to. It just popped somehow. I'm getting out of control—Butch named me for the right kind of bird. Canaries never get out of their cages, do they, Eva?

EVA: Jim! Don't be a fool.

JIM: Naw, they die in 'em—singin' sweetly till doomsday! God damn!

EVA [*brushing her hat*]: Speaking of birds—I wish the pigeons would be a little more careful! Don't you think it's a nice hat, Jim?

JIM [*without looking*]: Yes, colossal.

EVA: I bought it on the way home. I felt sort of gay and irresponsible—knowing tomorrow was the last day, I suppose! Jim! [*She catches his arm: he averts his face.*]

JIM [*his fear visible*]: If I get turned down again this time, I'll never get another chance.

EVA: Why not?

JIM: Because I'll blow-up! —Crack to pieces! I'm drawn as tight as I can get right now!

EVA: Don't be a damn fool, Jim.

JIM: You know what it's been like. Hated like poison for ten years by everybody but him. Working for him and all the time hating him so that it made me sick at the guts to look at him even! Ten years of being his stooge. Jimmy boy, do this, do that! Yes, Sir. Yes, Mr. Whalen! —My hands aching to catch that beefy red neck of his and choke the breath out of it! That's one reason why they shake so much—and here's another. Standing here at this window, looking out, seeing the streets, the buildings, the traffic moving, the lights going off and on, and me being pent up here, in these walls, locked in 'em so tight it's like I was buried under the earth in a coffin with a glass lid that I could see the world through! While I felt the worms crawling inside me. . .

EVA: No. Don't be a fool. [*She crosses upstage to the window.*] It's nice out. Gotten cooler

JIM: You said that before.

EVA [*smiling desperately*]: Well, it's still true. There's a carnival on South Bay. I ran in like a kid and took a ride on the zebra!

JIM: Yes?

EVA: There's two seats on the zebra, Jim. One in front, one in back— Next month we'll ride him together!

JIM [*suddenly breaking*]: Eva! Eva! [*He covers his face.*]

EVA [*running to him*]: I love you!

[*Pause.*]

JIM [*his voice choking*]: What is this place? What's it for? Why, why! The judges say guilty. But what is guilty? What does that word mean, anyhow? It's funny, but I don't know. [*He picks up the dictionary.*] Look it up in *Webster's Dictionary*. What's it say? "Responsible for the commission of crime." But why responsible? What's responsible mean? Who's ever been given a choice? When they mix up all the little molecules we're made out of, do they ask each one politely which he will be— rich man, poor man, beggar man, thief? God, no! It's all accidental. And yet the Judge says, "Jim, you're guilty!" [*He tosses the dictionary to the floor.*] This book's no good anymore. We need a new one with a brand new set of definitions.

EVA: Don't say any more—I won't let you! [*She kisses him.*]

JIM: How did this happen between you and me?

EVA: I don't know.

JIM: It's the dirtiest trick they've played on us yet.

EVA: Don't say that!

JIM: We can't have each other. We never can, Eva.

EVA: We can!

JIM: Where?

EVA: Somewhere.

JIM: How?

EVA: I don't know how.

JIM: Neither do I.

EVA: But next month—

JIM: There won't be any next month!

EVA: There will, oh, there will, there must be!

JIM: Why? —Why?

EVA: Because I love you so much that it's got to happen the way I want it to happen!

JIM: Why do you love me?

EVA: Why is anything on earth? I don't know why.

JIM: Neither do I—

[*They cling together in tortured ecstasy. Blackout. The lights come up as the phone rings.*]

JIM: Yes? I'll tell him. [*He hangs up.*]

EVA: What is it?

JIM: Schultz. They won't eat.

EVA: What's he going to do?

JIM: He's already got his instructions from Whalen. They'll be in Klondike at seven.

EVA [*pausing*]: I won't be down here tomorrow.

JIM: No?

EVA: I'll be in the newspaper offices. And at City Hall. Any place where people will listen!

JIM: You think they'll listen anywhere, Eva?

EVA: I'll make them listen!

JIM: And afterwards what will you do? With no job?

EVA: I'll only have to wait three weeks. And then I'll be *your* responsiblity, Jim!

JIM: I hope to God you're right.

EVA: I am! I know I am!

[*Whalen enters.*]

WARDEN: Hello! Still here, Jim?

JIM: Yes, Sir. Schultz called. They wouldn't eat supper.

WARDEN: Well—he's got his instructions.

JIM: Yes, he said that he had.

WARDEN [*scribbling on a piece of paper*]: Take this down to the switchboard and have it posted there and sent to all stations.

JIM: Does this mean—?

WARDEN: Never mind what it means. Just take it down there. And step lively!

JIM: Yes, Sir.

[*Jim goes out.*]

WARDEN [*to Eva*]: Back on the job, huh?

EVA: Yes.

WARDEN [*belching and removing his coat*]: I should have told you to bring some things with you.

EVA: What things?

WARDEN: Your little silk nightie and stuff.

EVA: What do you mean?

WARDEN: Quarantine! A bad epidemic's broken out! Twenty-five cases are going to be running a pretty high fever tonight so I've put this place under quarantine restrictions—nobody's gonna leave the grounds till the epidemic is over.

EVA: I can't stay here.

WARDEN [*busy with papers*]: Sure you can. My wife'll fix a room for you. You'll be very comfortable here.

EVA: No, I won't do it.

WARDEN: You've got no choice in the matter.

EVA: Haven't I?

WARDEN: Naw, I'm not running a risk on any outside inter-
ference while this trouble is going on. It's my business, I'm
going to keep it my business. So just as a routine precaution
I've ordered the boats to take no passengers on or off the island
without my special permission.

EVA: I think you're exceeding your authority.

WARDEN: Naw, you're wrong there. Times of emergency I can
do what I damn please. Say—what are you worried about?

EVA [frightened]: I—

WARDEN: I know. It's a nervous strain we've all been under
these last few days. I got gas on the stomach myself. Here. [He
pours a shot of whiskey.]

EVA: No, you've been drinking too much. I'm afraid it's af-
fected your sense of judgment. You ought to know you can't
get away with a thing like this!

WARDEN: Hey, now—look here!

EVA [excitedly]: I'm not a prisoner—I'm free to go and do as
I please—you can't stop me!

WARDEN: Look here, now!

[She grasps the phone.]

EVA: Riverside 3854 W! Riverside 3–8   [*She realizes the phone is cut off.*]

WARDEN: No out-going calls can get through. You're wasting your time.

EVA: Then I—I *am* a prisoner here!

WARDEN: You're temporarily detained on the island—might as well make the best of it! [*He pours another drink.*]

EVA: Oh!

WARDEN: Here, now, what's wrong with you?

EVA: I don't know why, but I'm terribly frightened.

WARDEN [*soothingly*]· You've gone and worked yourself up. There's nothing for you to be nervous about.

EVA: You! I'm afraid of you! [*She backs away from him.*]

WARDEN: Me? Why should you be scared of me?

EVA: I am, though. I'm scared to death of you. You've got to let me go, I can't stay with you any longer, Mr. Whalen.

WARDEN: Now, now.

EVA: No, don't touch me! Please don't.

WARDEN: You're hysterical, Eva.

EVA: Yes!

WARDEN [*purring*]: My wife gets spells like that, too—that "don't touch me" stuff!

EVA [*retreating.*]: Yes!

WARDEN: I know a good treatment for it that always works. There, now little girl you just take it easy. Relax. You're all worked up over nothing. You're stiff, see? Your nerves and your muscles are all drawn up real tight.

EVA: Yes. . . [*She has nearly collapsed with nervous exhaustion—his purring voice has a hypnotic effect.*]

WARDEN: Mmm. Now when my wife gets like this, I—I rub my fingers along her throat—real, real gently—till all the stiffness goes out. . .

EVA [*her eyes falling shut*]: Yes. . .

WARDEN [*gazes at her lasciviously*]: . . . and then I—

[*Eva sighs as though asleep*]

WARDEN: Eva? —Eva? [*He rises and opens the inner door, then hesitates—*]

[*The phone rings.*]

For Chrissakes, what is it now? Yeah? What? I'm coming right down there now!— [*He hangs up—purring drunkenly.*] You wait, li'l girl, I'll be right back in here! Yes, Siree. . . [*He fumbles into his coat and goes out.*]

[*Eva gasps as the door slams shut—she slowly rises. The outer door opens— Eva screams— Jim enters.*]

EVA: Jim! Jim!

[*Jim catches her in his arms.*]

Get me out of here, oh, please, *please*, get me out of here! [*She sobs wildly.*]

JIM: Hold on to yourself! [*He shakes her.*] Hold on to yourself!

EVA: I'm trying to, Jim.

JIM: Take a deep breath. Here—at the window.

EVA: Yes!

JIM: See those lights over there?

EVA: Yes!

JIM: That's the Lorelei on her way out. Be real quiet and you can hear the music. [*She leans against him—faint music is heard.*] Better now?

EVA: Yes. Thanks, Jim.

JIM: What happened? Just tell me real quietly and don't get excited about it.

EVA: He told me I—I'm a prisoner here! I can't leave! I don't know why, but it made me terribly frightened all of a sudden. His eyes, the way he looked at me, Jim—I had a feeling that something awful was going to happen—

JIM: Easy, now!

EVA: Yes. I guess I'm an awful sissy.

JIM: No, you've got more guts than me.

EVA: He—he came real close to me—and his voice—sort of put me to sleep.

JIM: Did he—?

EVA: No! He only opened that door. And then a bell rang—I could hear it like it was a thousand miles off!

JIM: A bell?

EVA: They called him upstairs, I guess. He left the room and I—I would have jumped out the window if you hadn't come just then!

JIM: There's nothing but water out there.

EVA: I didn't care. I just wanted to get away somehow.

JIM: You'll get away.

EVA: With you, Jim? You'll take me?

JIM: Yes. In a while. Don't you feel the walls shaking? They can't hold up much longer. There's too much boiling inside them—hate, torture, madness, fury! They'll blow wide open in a little while and we'll be loose!

EVA: I want to be with you when that happens! I want you to hold me like this—so that when the walls start falling I won't be crushed down under them, Jim.

JIM: We'll be together.

EVA: Where?

JIM: Meet me tonight in the southwest corner of the yard.

EVA: Will we be safe there?

JIM [*in a whisper*]: It's dark. Nobody could see us.

BLACKOUT—END OF ACT TWO

ACT THREE

Announcer: "Morning of August 15!"

A spot comes up on the office. The warden is at the phone. During the following episodes the theater is filled almost constantly with the soft hiss of live steam from the radiators—

WARDEN: Schultz? How hot is it down there now? 125? What's the matter? Git it up to 130! You got Butch O'Fallon in No. 3 aintcha? Okay, give No. 3 135 and don't let up on it till you git instructions from me. Hey! Got them windows in the hall shut? Good. Keep 'em shut an' let 'em squawk their goddamn heads off!

[*Blackout. A spot comes up on Klondike. The torture cell is seen through a scrim to give a misty or steam-clouded effect to the atmosphere. The men are sprawled on the floor, breathing heavily, their shirts off, skin shiny with sweat. A ceiling light glares relentlessly down on them. The walls are bare and glistening wet. Along them are radiators from which rise hissing clouds of live steam.*]

JOE [*coughing*]: W'at time is it?

BUTCH: How in hell would I know?

SWIFTY [*whimpering*]: Water—water.

JOE: I wonder if we been in here all night.

BUTCH: Sure we have. I can see daylight through the hole.

JOE: How long was you in that time?

137

BUTCH: Thirty-six hours.

JOE: Christ!

BUTCH: Yeah. And we've just done about eight.

SWIFTY: Water!

BUTCH: Hey! Y'know what—what the old maid said to the burglar when she—she found him trying to jimmy th' lock on th'—

JOE: Yeah. [*He coughs.*]

QUEEN: Swifty's sick. I am, too. Why don't somebody come here?

BUTCH: Aw, you heard that one?

JOE: Yeah. A long time ago, Butch. [*He coughs.*]

BUTCH: You oughta know some new ones.

JOE: Naw. Not any new ones, Butch.

BUTCH: Then tell some old ones, goddamn it!! Dontcha all lie there like you was ready to be laid under! Let's have some life in this party— Sing! Sing! You know some good songs, Queenie, you got a voice! C'mon you sons-of-guns! Put some pep in it! Sing it out, sing it out loud, boys! [*He sings wildly, hoarsely.*]

> Pack up your troubles in yuhr ole kit bag an'
> Smile, smile, smile!

[*The others join in feebly*—]

Sing it out! Goddamit, sing it out loud!

> What's the use of worrying
> It never was worthwhile!

[*Joe tries to sing—he is suddenly bent double in a paroxysm of coughing.*]

SWIFTY [*in a loud anguished cry*]: Water! Water! Water! [*He sobs.*]

[*There is a loud shrill hiss of steam from the radiators as more pressure is turned on.*]

QUEEN [*in frantic horror*]: *They're givin' us more*! Oh, my God, why don't they stop now! Why don't they let us out! Oh, Jesus, Jesus, please, please, please! [*He sobs wildly and falls on the floor.*]

SWIFTY [*weakly*]: Water—water. . .

BUTCH: Yeah. They're givin' us more heat. Sure, they're givin' us more heat. Dontcha know you're in Klondike? Aw, w'at's a use, yer crybabies. Yuh wanta go on suckin' a sugar-tit all yer life? Gwan, sing it out—

> I'm forever blowing BUBBLES!
> Pretty bubbles in the—AIR!

SHAPIRO: There is nothing to be done about it, nothing at all. I come of a people that are used to suffer. It is not a new thing. I have it in my blood to suffer persecution, misery, starvation, death.

SWIFTY: Water.

SHAPIRO [*mumbles in Yiddish, then*]: My head is full, full. Aching in here. Broken already, perhaps. Rose? Rose? You know the property on South Maple Street—it's all in your name, my darling—be careful—don't make bad investments—

JOE [*coughing*]: Lemme at the air hole.

QUEEN: You're hoggin' it!

JOE: Cantcha see I'm choking to death? [*He coughs.*]

[*The steam hisses louder.*]

BUTCH [*rising*]: We got to systematize this business. Quit fightin' over the air hole. The only air that's fit to breathe is comin' through there. We gotta take turns breathin' it. We done sixteen hours about. Maybe we'll do ten more, twenty more, thirty more.

JOE: Christ!

QUEEN: We can't make it!

BUTCH: We can if we organize. Keep close to the floor. Stay in a circle round the wall. Each guy take his turn. Fifteen seconds. Maybe later ten seconds or five seconds. I do the counting. And when a guy flips out—he's finished—he's through—push him outa the line— This ain't a first-aid station—this is Klondike—and by God—some of us are gonna beat it— Okay? Okay, Joe?

JOE: Yeah.

BUTCH: Well, git started then.

SWIFTY: Water!

BUTCH: Push the kid up here first.

[*They shove Swifty's inert body to the air hole.*]

Breathe! Breathe! Breathe, goddamn you, breathe! [*He jerks Swifty up by the collar—stares at his face.*] Naw, it's no use. I guess he's beating a cinder track around the stars now!

QUEEN: He ain't dead! Not yet! He's unconscious, Butch! Give him a chance!

BUTCH [*inexorably*]: Push him outa the line. [*As the lights dim. . .*] Okay—Shapiro—Joe—

[*Theme up: "I'm Forever Blowing Bubbles." Fade.*]

DIM OUT

EPISODE TWO

Announcer: "Evening of August 15!"

A spot comes up on the office. Whalen is at the phone.

WARDEN: You heard 'em what? Singin! Well, give 'em somthing to sing about! 140? Git it up to 145 in Butch's compartment! You bet I want 'em left in there all night. Naw, keep the windows shut. Water? Let 'em make their own water!

[*Blackout. A spot comes up on Klondike. Swifty lies dead in center, a shirt over his face. The voices are hoarse, breathing more labored. Joe coughs wrackingly. The radiators hiss loudly.*]

BUTCH: Here comes more! Keep down! Keep down!

[*Queen sobs wildly. Shapiro mumbles in Yiddish*]

Joe! Look! I got it with me! [*He extracts a razor from his belt.*]

JOE: That's one way out.

BUTCH: Maybe the boss will come down here to look us over.

JOE [*coughing*]: Naw, he wouldn't.

BUTCH: Maybe Schultz will. Or the Canary. [*He rises.*] Schultz! Schultz! Naw, it's no dice, he's too yellow to stick his puss in here! But if he does ever—

[*A whistle sounds.*]

Hear that? It's the lock-up bell! We've done twenty-four hours, Joe. We only got twelve more to go!

142

JOE: How d'you know how long it will be?

BUTCH: They don't want to kill us!

JOE: Why don't they? [*He coughs.*] —Your turn, Butch.

BUTCH: Yeah, git moving, Queenie!

QUEEN: Naw! Lemme breathe!

[*Butch tears him away from air hole. Shapiro shouts something in Yiddish. Queen continues rising and staggering.*]

I got to get out of here! Lemme out, lemme out! [*He pounds at the wall, then staggers blindly towards the radiators.*]

BUTCH: Stay away from the radiators!

[*Queen staggers directly into the cloud of steam — screams — falls to the floor.*]

He's scalded himself.

[*Queen screams and sobs.*]

Stop it! Goddamn yuh— [*He grasps Queen's collar and cracks his head against floor.*] There now!

JOE: Butch—you killed him.

BUTCH: Somebody shoulda done him that favor a long time ago.

[*Shapiro mumbles in Yiddish.*]

You heard that one about—the niggers in church? "—Rastus, she says—Naw, he says—Mandy—Mandy how long does the Preacher—"

[*Dim out. A spot comes up on the office. Whalen is on the phone.*]

WARDEN: Schultz? How hot is it down there now in Butch's compartment? 150? Good! Keep it there till I give you further instructions— I'll be in my office till about midnight and if anything comes up—

[*Fade out. A spot comes up on Klondike. Shapiro, Queen, and Swifty are dead and lie in the center. Butch and Joe, gasping, crouch together by the air hole.*]

JOE: Butch—

BUTCH: Yeah.

JOE: Y'know that razor—

BUTCH: What about it?

JOE: Use it on me! Quick! I wanta get done with this!

BUTCH: Keep hold of yourself, Joe. You can make it.

JOE: Naw, I can't, Butch. I'm chokin' t' death. I can't stand it.

BUTCH: Breathe!

JOE: There ain't no air coming in now, Butch.

BUTCH: There's air—breathe it, Joe.

JOE: Naw. . .

[*Butch raises his face and shakes him.*]

BUTCH [*hoarsely*]: Goddamn yuh, don't chicken out! Stay with me, Joe! We can beat Klondike!

[*Joe laughs deliriously. Butch continues, springing up.*]

Turn off them fucking radiators!! Turn the heat off, goddamn yuh, turn it off! [*He staggers toward the radiators.*] Stop it, y'hear me? Quit that SSSS! SSSS! [*He imitates the hissing sound.*] I'll turn yuh off, yuh suns-a-bitches! [*He springs on the radiators and grapples with them as though with a human adversary—he tries to throttle steam with his hands—he's scalded—screams with agony—backs away, his face contorted, wringing his hands.*] SSSSS! SSSSS! SSSSS! [*He is crazily imitating their noise.*]

JOE: Christ, Butch, it ain't no good that way. You've blown your top. What's the percentage? [*Butch staggers back to the air hole.*]

BUTCH: Joe! Hey, Joe! Swifty! You, Queen! Shapiro! [*He tugs at one of the bodies.*] Let's sing! Let's all sing something! Sing it out! Loud!

For-tune's always hid-ing!

Why don't you bastards sing something! Come on—sing! Sing!

I looked ev'rywhere—!

[*The lights dim as the music completes the final lines of* "Bubbles."]

DIM OUT

EPISODE THREE

Announcer: *"The Southwest Corner of the Yard!"*

Dark stage and complete silence for several moments. Then—

EVA: Jim!

JIM: Here!

EVA: I'm late. I couldn't help it.

JIM: Shhh!

EVA [*lowering her voice*]: His wife's not on the Island. She left this afternoon. I can't stay there in that place with him, Jim, I can't do it!

JIM: Shhh. Don't talk.

EVA: What am I going to do, Jim? What am I going to do?

JIM: *Don't talk*! It's not safe. They might hear us. Eva—

[*Pause. The beam of a searchlight moves over them.*]

EVA: Jim! They're moving the light!

JIM: Shhh! Keep it down!

[*The light disappears.*]

EVA: Oh. Thank God.

JIM: Now!

FVA: You've never even said that you loved me.

JIM: I love you. Now!

EVA: Oh, Jim—Jim! [*A longer pause.*]

JIM: The light again!

[*It circles lower this time and pauses directly above them.*]

Christ! Keep down low!

EVA: Jim!

JIM: Crawl! No, that way! Quick!

[*The light suddenly moves down and shines full upon Eva's face. Eva screams. A siren sounds. Blackout. A spot comes up on the office. Jim and Eva are there with a Guard. Whalen enters.*]

WARDEN: What *is* this?

GUARD: It looks like the Canary's turned into a lovebird, Mr. Whalen.

WARDEN: Aw!

GUARD: I heard a noise in the southwest corner of the yard. Sounded like a girl's voice. I dropped the light on—there they was!

WARDEN: Aw! Doing what?

GUARD: Well, they weren't picking daisies.

WARDEN: Aw! [*To Eva.*]: You a while ago. Got hysterical in here. Objected because there wasn't no chaperone in the house. Then you run out there like a bitch in heat and—

JIM [*starting forward*]: Stop it!

WARDEN: Aw!

JIM: It's easy to say things like that when you've got a gun stuck in my back.

WARDEN: Put the gun down. [*He takes a rubber hose from the hall.*] It's disillusioning what happens when you put too much confidence in the wrong people. Take your coat off.

EVA: No, you can't do that to him. I won't stand for it. It wasn't his fault. I asked him to meet me out there. Because I was scared. Scared of you! Scared of this awful place you've got us locked up in! And now you let us out! You let us both out of here now! Before I scream! I'll let the whole world know what's going on here!

WARDEN: Take hold of that girl!

JIM [*springing toward them*]: Let her go!

[*Whalen flails at Jim with the hose. Jim staggers to the floor, covering his face. Eva screams and struggles.*]

WARDEN: Take him out of here!

GUARD: Where to?

WARDEN: Klondike! Throw him in there with Butch O'Fallon! They're real good friends! [*He laughs.*]

[*The guard goes out dragging Jim.*]

Well, Eva—

[*Eva turns her face sharply away.*]

I'm sorry about this whole thing. I mean it sincerely. What I just said—forget that! You probably don't stop to realize what a strain I've been under. It's not easy to be the head of an institution like this. I've handled it like I would handle anything else. The best I knew how. Sometimes—I'm telling you the truth, girl—I've been so sick at heart at things I've had to do and see done—that it hurt me to look into my own little girl's face and hear her call me—Daddy! [*He pours himself a drink.*] Here. You take one, too. [*He is breathing heavily and for the moment is perfectly in earnest.*] Maybe it's done something to me in here. [*He touches his head.*] Sometimes I don't feel quite the same anymore. Awful, awful! Men down there now being subjected to awful torture! But what can I do about it? I got to keep discipline—dealing with criminals—there's no other way— Take your drink.

EVA: Thank you. [*She takes it.*]

WARDEN: There's two ways I could look at this. It could be a serious business. By your own confession you—you remember what you said, you—had Jim meet you out in the yard— Now I'm inclined to be broad-minded about such things—these discrepancies in the commissary report— [*He shrugs and smiles.*] —things like that—serious sometimes—at least they can look that way—

EVA: What do you mean, Mr. Whalen? You mean you would—try to accuse me of—!

WARDEN: No, no, no! [*He smiles engagingly.*] Not unless you forced me to.

EVA: What do you want?

WARDEN: What does any man want? What did Jim want, what did you give him? —Sympathy!

EVA: Oh.

WARDEN: That way it could be very simple. We're all of us nervous, strained, overwrought! —Sympathy! All of us need it!

EVA: Oh. What will you do to Jim now?

WARDEN: Well—

EVA: I love him! You probably don't understand how it happened between us— He's coming up for parole next month.

WARDEN: Yes, I have the letter in my desk now.

EVA: What letter?

WARDEN: Recommending Jim's—release! Of course after this—

EVA: You won't send it?

WARDEN: Well—

EVA: Suppose I—I did sympathize as you say—and—and kept my mouth shut and anything else that you want! Would you send the letter? Would Jim get his parole?

WARDEN [*smiling*]: Why not? [*He laughs gently.*] You see how easy it is to straighten things out!

EVA: Now? Would you send it now?

WARDEN: Now? It's—pretty late now—

EVA: The mailboat leaves at eleven-forty-five. You could have it sent over by that. Don't worry. I won't back out. I'm not afraid of you now. I like you—I'd like to show you how much!

[*The Warden removes the letter from the drawer and rings the bell. A guard enters.*]

WARDEN: Put this in the mail.

GUARD: Yes, Sir. [*He goes out.*]

WARDEN: My head aches, aches all the time—my wife's left me—the little girl, too— [*He opens the inner door.*] We're all of us nervous and tired, overwrought! Aren't we? Yes—[*He ushers Eva in as the light fades.*]

DIM OUT

Announcer: "The Showdown"

A spot comes up on Klondike. Butch lies by the air hole. The bodies of the others are heaped in the center—Butch is apparently unconscious. Voices are heard in the hall. Butch slowly raises his head, becomes tense.

SCHULTZ [*as the door opens*]: —makin' love to the Boss's secretary out in the yard—fancy that!

[*Butch rolls over quickly and feigns unconsciousness.*]

Whew! What a stink! Hey—Chick! C'mere! Steam's s' goddamn thick I can't see nothin'. Gimme that flash—

CHICK: Looks t' me like—Jeez! They're *stiffs*!

SCHULTZ: Stiffs! Y'mean—

CHICK: Roasted! Roasted alive! God Almighty! I didn't know nothin' like this was going on in here.

SCHULTZ: Shut up! How many are there?

[*During this Butch has slowly risen and poised himself for attack.*]

Gimme the flash! Shapiro, Joe—Swifty—The Queen— Where's Butch?

BUTCH [*springing*]: Here! Here! [*He clutches Schultz by the throat.*]

[*Jim attacks Chick. A shot is fired; Jim wrests the revolver from the guard.*]

JIM: Toss your mittens!

BUTCH [*slowly releasing Schultz*]: Aw! You! The Canary!

SCHULTZ [*uncertainly*]: Good work, Jim!

JIM: I mean you, Schultz! Reach high! Butch—get them keys off him!

BUTCH [*slowly grinning*]: Aw—aw! [*He snatches the keys.*]

SCHULTZ: What is this?

JIM: Butch—let the boys out! We're going upstairs!

BUTCH: Yeah!

SCHULTZ: You'll get the hot seat for this! Every mother's bastard of you will! What are you going to do, Jim?

JIM: Get into something comfortable, Schultz! You're going to SWEAT!

[*Jim backs out and slams the door. Schultz rushes to it, pounds and screams. Blackout. The stage is dark for a moment. There is the long wail of a siren. A spot comes up in the Warden's office. Whalen steps out of the inner room—he listens, tense with alarm. —The office door is thrown open—Jim enters.*]

WARDEN: Jim!

JIM [*his clothes torn and bloody from the earlier beating*]: Yeah! Sometimes even hell breaks open and the damned get loose!

WARDEN: What's happened—downstairs? [*He edges back—pushes a buzzer.*]

JIM: No use pushing that. There's nobody on the other end of it.

WARDEN: They've broken out of—Klondike?

JIM: Yes. All of 'em but four. Four didn't break out cause they're dead—but they sent their regards to you, Boss, they want to be remembered!

WARDEN: How did you get that? [*He points to the revolver.*]

JIM: Raided the munitions!

WARDEN: What happened to Schultz?

JIM: He got in trouble downstairs, he's locked in Klondike, keeping the dead boys company down there— The other screws are locked up in the cellblock. Stand outa the way. [*He removes a revolver from the desk.*] Where's the girl?

WARDEN: She—left.

JIM: You're sure of that.

WARDEN: Yes— Why?

JIM: This ain't a safe place to be right now.

WARDEN: Look here, Jim—

JIM: What's the matter? You don't look good.

WARDEN: I'll make a deal with you—where are the boys?

JIM [*jerking his thumb toward the door*]: Waiting out there at the gate. I wanted to make sure the girl wasn't here before I let 'em come in.

WARDEN: Naw! You can't do that!

JIM: Sure. I'm the reception committee. I've got the keys.

[*Men are heard shouting outside. Eva appears at the inner door.*]

JIM: Eva!

EVA: Jim, don't do it, Jim! It's no use— He's written a letter asking for your parole, he sent it already!

WARDEN: Yes, Jim. I done it just now, because she—

JIM: Because she—what? [*He looks at them both.*] Aw! Get back inside there, Eva.

[*The boss starts to follow. Jim jerks him back.*]

Naw, you stay out here!

EVA: Jim! [*He forces her inside and locks the door.*]

WARDEN: Jim, you wouldn't give up your parole for the chair?

JIM: Sure. It's worth it. I haven't forgotten.

WARDEN: Forgotten—what?

JIM: Twenty-one days in the Hole. Dr. Jones.

WARDEN [*following him to door*]: Afterwards I was your friend!

JIM: I wasn't yours!

WARDEN [*nearly screaming*]: I was good to you afterwards, Jim!

JIM: I still had your signature on my back! Now we've got a new whipping-boss waiting out there—Butch O'Fallon!

WARDEN: Naw! Jim! Jim!

[*Jim has gone out—the roar of the men rises as doors are opened. The Warden gasps and darts behind the desk— Men enter like a pack of wolves and circle about the walls.*]

BUTCH [*lunging through*]: Where is he?

WARDEN: Butch!

BUTCH [*his eyes blinded*]: There! I've caught the smell of him now!

[*The two rulers face each other for the first time. Outside there is scattered gunfire, and a flickering light is thrown through the windows like the reflection of flames.*]

It's been you an' me a long time—you in here—me out there— But now it's—together at last— It's a pleasure, pig face, to make your acquaintance!

WARDEN: Look here now, boys—O'Fallon—Jim—I'll make a deal with you all— You've got to remember now—I've got the United States army in back of me!

BUTCH [*laughing and coming toward him*]: You've got that wall in back of you— Where's the Doctor?

CONVICT: Here! [*He snatches the rubber hose from the wall and hands it to Butch.*]

BUTCH: Yeah!

WARDEN: Naw! Think of the consequences! Don't be fools!

[*Butch strikes him with the hose.*]

WARDEN [*cowering to the floor*]: Stop! I'm a family man! I've got a wife! A daughter! A little—*girrrrl!* [*The final word turns into a scream of anguish as Butch crouches over him with the whip beating him with demoniacal fury till he is senseless.*]

[*The siren of an approaching boat is heard.*]

CONVICT: What is it?

ANOTHER: Gunboat!

ANOTHER: Troopers!

ANOTHER: They're landing!

ANOTHER: Douse the glims!

[*The room is plunged into total darkness except for the weird flickering of flame shadows on the walls— Men begin a panicky exodus from the room.*]

VOICES: Git down there— Fight 'em off— Troopers! —Not a chance— No chance anyhow! —You wanta go back to Klondike? —Fight! —Sure, fight! —We got nothing to lose! [*Names are shouted—gates clang—machine gun fire is heard.*]

[*The noise becomes remote and dream-like—the room is almost quiet except for the distant, sad wail of the siren which continues endlessly (like the voice of damnation at the palace gates).*]

JIM: What have you done to him?

BUTCH: Thrown his blubbering carcass out the window.

JIM: Into the water?

BUTCH: Yeah. Straight down.

JIM: Butch—we've got a chance that way.

BUTCH: Swim for it? Naw, not me. I don't know how to swim. Besides it's half a mile to shore and rough as hell.

JIM: What will you do?

BUTCH: Stay here and fight it out.

JIM: I think I'll take my chances with the water.

BUTCH [*slowly extending his hand*]: Good luck, I had you figured wrong.

JIM: Thanks.

BUTCH [*pulling off ring*]: Here. There used to be a girl named Goldie at the Paradise Dance Hall on Brook Street west of the Ferry. If you should ever meet her, give her this— And tell her that I—kept it—all this time.

JIM: Sure, Butch—I will if I make—

BUTCH [*going to the door*]: So long.

[*Rapid gunfire and distant shouting heard outside. Jim unlocks the inner door.*]

JIM: Eva.

[*Eva comes out slowly— she falls sobbing on his shoulder.*]

JIM: Don't cry!

EVA: No. I won't. There'd be no use in that. Jim, you were right about the pyrotechnical display!

JIM: Stand back from the window!

EVA [*hysterically gay*]: It's lovely, isn't it, Jim!

JIM: Yes, lovely as hell!

EVA: What did they do to him? —Whalen?

JIM [*thumb to window*]: The fish will have indigestion.

EVA: Jim! Have you thought what you'll get for this?

JIM: Nothing. They won't have a chance.

EVA: What are you going to do?

[*Sound cue: faint music.*]

JIM: There's water out that window. I can swim.

EVA: No, Jim, there's not a chance that way.

JIM: A chance? What's that? I never heard of it! [*On this speech he slowly approaches the window over the sea.*] Hear that? That music! It's—

EVA: The Lorelei!

JIM: The Lorelei— [*He tears off his coat.*] Now I retract those unkind things I said!

EVA: What will you do?

JIM: Swim out and catch a ride!

EVA: You couldn't, Jim— They'd bring you back— They wouldn't let you go!

JIM: They'll never see me.

EVA: Why?

JIM: Don't ask me why! There'll be a rope or something hanging over the side. Or if she doesn't ride too high I'll grab the rail! How! Don't ask me how! Now is the time for unexpected things, for miracles, for wild adventures like the storybooks!

EVA: Oh, Jim, there's not a chance that way!

JIM: Almost a chance! I've heard of people winning on a long shot. And if I don't —At least I'll be outside!

EVA: Oh, Jim I would have liked to live with you outside. We might have found a place where searchlights couldn't point their fingers at us when we kissed. I would have given you so much you've never had. Quick love is hard. It gives so little pleasure. We should have had long nights together with no walls. Or no *stone* walls —I know the place! A tourist camp beside a highway, Jim, with all night long the great trucks rumbling by—but only making shadows through the blinds! I'd touch the stone you're made of, Jim, and make you warm, so warm, so terribly warm your love would burn a scar upon my body that no length of time could heal! —Oh, Jim, If we could meet like that, at some appointed time, some place decided now, where we could love in secret and be warm, protected, not afraid of things— We could forget all this as something dreamed! —Where shall it be? When, Jim? Tell me before you go!

JIM: Quick! It's almost close enough! Get that shoe off!

EVA [*pulling off his shoes*]: Yes Jim! But tell me where?

JIM [*climbing to the sill*]: Watch the personal columns!

EVA: Jim! —Good-bye! [*He plunges from the window.*] — Good-bye. . .

[*Music from the Lorelei swells. Flame-shadows brighten on the walls. Shouting and footsteps are heard. Troopers rush in.*]

ONE [*switching on light.*]: A girl—

TWO: The Warden's Secretary!

THREE [*crossing to her*]: You're all right, sister. [*To others*]: She's dazed, can't talk— Get her a drink, somebody.

ONE: What's that she's got?

THREE: A pair of—shoes!

ONE: Whose are they? What's she doing with them?

EVA [*facing the window with a faint smile*]: I picked them up somewhere. I can't remember.

[*Light fades except for a spot on Eva, clutching Jim's shoes. Music from the Lorelei rises to a crescendo as a string of colored lights slides past the window. Dim out.*]

LOUD-SPEAKER: Aw there, it is! Y'can see it now, folks. That's the Island! Sort of misty tonight on account of the moon's gone under. Them walls are *escape-proof*, folks. Thirty-five hundred men locked in there an' some of them gonna stay there till Doomsday— [*Music.*] —Ah, music again! Dancing on the upper deck, folks, dancing, —dancing. . .

[*Musical theme up.*]

THE END

A SELECTED LIST OF
METHUEN MODERN PLAYS

All Methuen Drama books are available through mail order or from your local bookshop.

Please send cheque/eurocheque/postal order (sterling only) Access, Visa, Mastercard, Diners Card, Switch or Amex.

☐☐☐☐☐☐☐☐☐☐☐☐☐☐

Expiry Date:_____ Signature: _____

Please allow 75 pence per book for post and packing U.K.
Overseas customers please allow £1.00 per copy for post and packing.

ALL ORDERS TO:
Methuen Books, Books by Post, TBS Limited, The Book Service, Colchester Road, Frating Green, Colchester, Essex CO7 7DW.

NAME: _____

ADDRESS: _____

Please allow 28 days for delivery. Please tick box if you do not
wish to receive any additional information ☐

Prices and availability subject to change without notice.